Jack Lenor Larsen

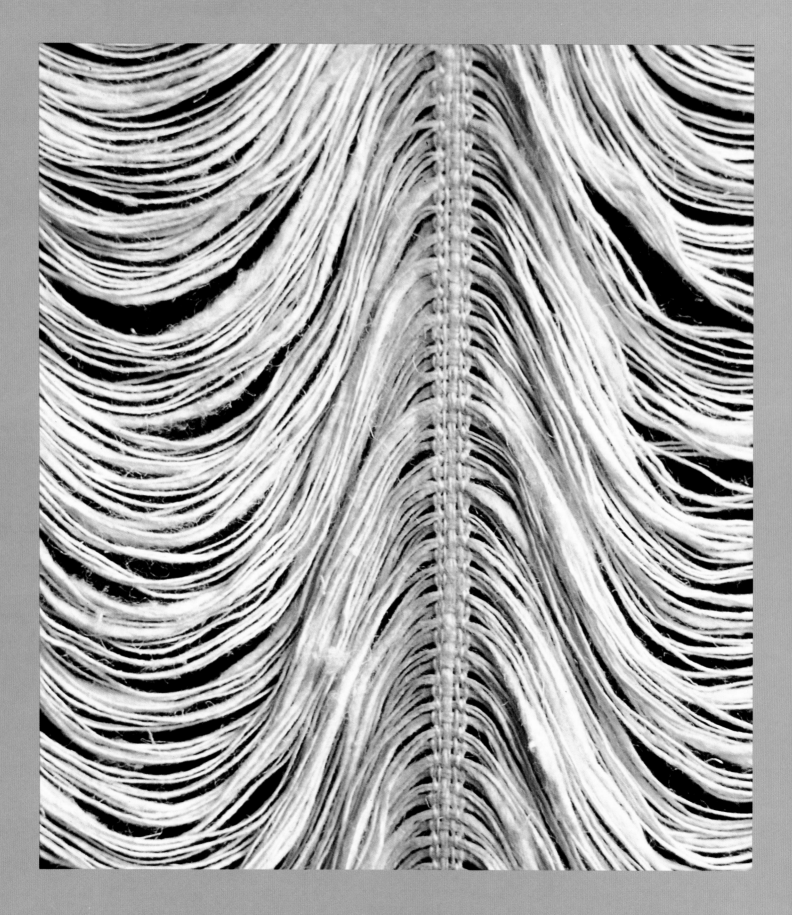

Jack Lenor Larsen

A Weaver's Memoir

By Jack Lenor Larsen

HARRY N. ABRAMS, INC., PUBLISHERS

Dedicated to my mother,
Mabel Larsen, 1903–1998

EDITOR   Elisa Urbanelli
DESIGNER   Ellen Nygaard Ford

Library of Congress Cataloging-in-Publication Data

Larsen, Jack Lenor.
    Jack Lenor Larsen—a weaver's memoir / by Jack Lenor Larsen.
            p.   cm.
    Includes index.
    ISBN 0-8109-3589-9 (hardcover)
    1. Larsen, Jack Lenor. 2. Men weavers—United States—Biography.
    I. Title.
    NK8998.L3A2   1998
    745.4'4'92— dc21   98-12989

Printed and bound in Japan

Harry N. Abrams, Inc.
100 Fifth Avenue
New York, N.Y. 10011
www.abramsbooks.com

Contents

The sixth of September 1945 was a fine day

on Puget Sound. As the morning fog lifted and the silver *Kalakala* churned

CHAPTER 1

The Early Years

about and steamed toward Seattle, the streamlined ferry faced directly into the

pink majesty of Mount Rainier. "Going to the mountain" seemed propitious;

my expectations were high that day as I moved onto the University of

Washington campus, back from Bremerton, the navy town an hour across the

sound, to Seattle's University District where I had spent my first six years.

The scene was splendid, as only Puget Sound in sunlight can be. Yet it is not sunlight

but water that makes this corner of the country what it is – water in a thousand

bays for fishing and sailing and for towing logjams; water to live by in houses peeking

out from fir-fringed shores, water making our soft gray clouds which, in turn, drench

In the early years Muggins and I enjoyed outings at Juanita Beach, north of Seattle.

the green foothills choked with Douglas fir. From the snow-capped Olympic and Cascade Mountains this water plummets to the sound in dozens of salmon rivers with Indian names like Duckabush, Ho, and Hama Hama. This water-soaked greenness was called God's Country by settlers from New England and Norway, prospectors from the Yukon, and farmers from Japan, as well as my parents, who came to Seattle from the Canadian prairies of Alberta before I was born.

From the ferry dock I had watched – without envy – schoolboys swimming from an anchored sailboat. I was shedding all the carefree, irresponsible summer days of swimming and spearfishing as though they were soiled linen. My boat was moving and I was glad; at the university there would be an unknown "something" of which I wanted more. Manhood and independence? Yes. The world? yes! And life.

As the ferry approached, the Seattle skyline rose high in front of us, not because the buildings were so tall, but rather because the successive blocks are arranged in tiers up the steepness of First Hill like schoolchildren posed on steps for a class picture. Now that the wartime blackout was lifted, some of the lights were on; the sight was impressive. At the foot of the hill were long piers; to the south, Todd Shipyards; then, farther to the east, the expansive Boeing plants. Of course it was not a "great" city, but to all those like myself, coming in from that sparsely populated region north of San Francisco and west of Minnesota, this was the Queen City and a place of promise.

As a boy I had always built things: boats and houses, gardens and crafts. The house in Bremerton that we moved to when I started high school had been built for an art teacher who commissioned a fine interior designer. Finally married, the owner took away only some books and clothes, leaving us distinguished furnishings and a decade of subscriptions to *Vanity Fair*, *House & Garden*, and *Vogue*. My reading on rainy days of such writers as T. H. Robsjohn-Gibbings and Elsa Maxwell opened my eyes to a cosmopolitan world that was very appealing. Even more extraordinary were the books by Frank Lloyd Wright. Both his prescriptions for a sensible modernity and his drawings whetted my appetite to a life beyond middle-class conventions.

As I began college, I was not certain whether it was architecture or landscapes or furniture I most wanted to make. I had enrolled in architecture. The university's School of Architecture was at the time considered one of the best in the country, perhaps because of architects Welton Becket and Minoru Yamasaki and furniture maker George Nakashima, as well as the local men creating the Northwest Style. School was good; I learned to work, to concentrate, and to care. In the second year it was furniture design and interior design, taught by Hope Foote in the art department, that attracted me. Taste, refinement, and a whole expanding world reached out before me. Painters within the department were dominated by Cézannesque structure, but outside were Mark Tobey, Morris Graves, and Kenneth Callahan, whose paintings grew out of the landscape. Their world was the one I knew and wanted to approximate in whatever I did.

Elsewhere on campus, the faculty had been enriched by an influx in the 1920s of rebellious East Coast intellectuals. There were also quiet, wise minds from China. My personal break-through was first mixed up with drama and contemporary arts, later with anthropology and philosophy. We were lucky to be students in these postwar years, when there was fervor about art, about design. Especially in those areas related to architecture, there was a belief that design would transform humdrum decorum.

Growing out of this spirit, with neither pretense nor con-vention, the Northwest house seemed right. Sensibly facing the view, it was often perched on a hillside, surrounded by trees and stained-out olive-gray to become part of the hill itself. Whether they stood tall and plentiful or became lumber encasing framed forms, our pointed firs were important. As architecture students, we were concerned with wood finishes and bleaches, with wood rough sawed or vertically grained, wood for walls, ceilings, and floors. The Northwest house, as evolved in the forties by Pietro Belluschi and John Yeon, differed from the International Style of Southern California in that its rain-shedding roofs usually were low and gabled. Basically, its one-story rectangle was related to the local Indian longhouse, with a deep overhang and fenestration based on the modular logic of stud construction, elements not out of place in Kyoto.

We made pilgrimages to Portland. In the 1940s, an older, mellower Oregon offered such breakthroughs as the Equitable Building, Belluschi's curtain-walled high-rise, which was one of the first International Style towers in America. His Portland Museum was bringing in major shows of contemporary art and soon adding the great Rasmussen Collection of Native American Art. In Portland, too, Norman Yeon opened the first contempo-rary design shop while the Oregon Ceramic Studio (now the Contemporary Crafts Association) encouraged craftsmen in a five-state area. It was here I would have my first one-man show.

By the time this photo was taken the family triangle felt better balanced: My parents were a pair but I, at fifteen, felt less dependent on their approval.

Perhaps more than anything else, the regional culture was Japanese, or at least Oriental. Out there on the very edge of the continent, the Orient seemed as close as the American East. Our professors had traveled and studied there; painters like Tobey and Graves returned from Japan with an Oriental mystique. The Oriental collections at the Seattle Art Museum contributed to the culture, as did our sizable Asian population. So did the climate: our sunless skies, mountains, sea, and foggy evergreens seemed more akin to a Japanese landscape than to the cow-filled, red-maple country on *Saturday Evening Post* covers.

PARENTAL INFLUENCES

Because parental influences began early and still continue, I have usually been unaware of their power. From both parents I sensed a need for preparedness – what could be done ahead would be at the ready. Mother shopped once a week for all meals, including those for unexpected company. Dad would not think of being at the job or in his boat without all the gear possibly needed, just as he sized up situations so as to be in full command. These early influences had been the regimen I assiduously resisted, or slowly learned. There was a place for everything and a set time for weekly tasks, such as laundry. It was only when off to my own digs at the university that an urge for order kicked in. Freed of my mother's presence, I took on her sense of unrelenting order. If I had been slow in acquiring Dad's skills, at least I understood their value. He built houses. I had built houses too, of any materials available and with any help I could muster. What I did not learn from Dad was his charm or his easy, teasing ways of relating to people in all walks of life. At work and at play he was a winner, inspiring me to someday do *something* remarkably well.

How little has changed since the days when I dreamed up weekend projects or excursions! Then as now, I anticipated the steps to realize my projects. What materials, tools, or provisions, what sequence of steps, what helpmates, and with what result? Pleasure in the doing, of course, was the objective; or was it the camaraderie?

Knowing Mother as a widow was an incomparable lesson. Neither aggressive nor particularly assertive, she had needed to control her only child and a husband who became indolent after retirement. With both of us gone, all her focus was devoted to others. While she had strength there were friends' plantings to put in, or spring and fall garden cleanups. What meals could she send over to shut-ins, or what calls and gifts to nursing homes? As her energy ebbed she still continued to think of others' needs. Never overtly religious, she nonetheless adopted her own mother's adherence to the Golden Rule.

TIME

As a Depression child I was taught by example that time, like money, is not to be wasted. A prime way of accomplishing this was to compartmentalize time in the way that Mother's kitchen and Dad's tackle boxes were compactly arranged for easy access. Days of the week were scheduled for particular chores, seasons determined by when fruit came in or the salmon were running. With this schedule cast in stone, spontaneity was the more welcome. Even though we all had telephones, friends' dropping in was still so common that one was always prepared for these happy occasions. This practice, of course, led to disappointments when the would-be hosts were not in or already had guests, but houses were always spotless, flowers arranged, cookie jars and larders stocked. Fruit cupboards and coolers (later freezers) were so ample one could go without shopping for a week or take in a large group for supper without warning. So, all the more reason that chores, including homework, be done in good time. Waste not, want not; be prepared!

In summers, from the time I was eight until about twelve, Dad would invariably come home Friday afternoons asking, "Shall we go fishing?" Food hampers were quickly packed, tackle stowed in his sturdy boat, and off we would go to Hansville, just an hour north, where salmon of some sort always seemed plentiful. As the men were up and out to sea before dawn, then back out at dusk, I had long days to build sand castles or explore the beach for miles in either direction. Twice daily there was an opportunity to ride the breakers from passing Princess ships going to and from Victoria. When the *Empress of China* would pass en route to Yokohama, I dreamed of being a stowaway – first in a lifeboat, then in a vacant stateroom.

Twenty-five-foot blackfish played on the surface of our cove, and gulls gathered to attack surfacing schools of herring. Here was the languor of long days stretched out in seemingly endless summer – on a larger, stormier canvas than at Phinney Bay, where I cast bottles with notes into the outgoing tide, or launched the dugout, kayak, and other craft I laboriously constructed and then sold.

Phinney Bay was round and so shallow that it was half-empty at minus tide, and full of warmed, wind-lapped water. This least fashionable of Bremerton's waterfront neighborhoods was where I learned to swim at six and swim across the bay at eight. There were four families of Andersons and other friends, an isolated Indian reservation nearby, a desert island, and beyond it a farm for peacocks and exotic fowl.

Walking north from our beach I found sand cliffs forming a point, with caves above and geoducks burrowed deeply within submerged reefs. Safe from digging, these ancient ten-pound clams could be counted on to surprise my unwary friends by spraying warm brine several feet over their bronzed young bodies! Beyond the point ran a narrows of cold, fast-moving water, forbidding to swimmers but fine for sailing. Above this headland were miles of wooded wilderness for exploration, gathering trilliums and red-currant blossoms in spring, huckleberries and wild blackberries come summer.

All this was mine and mine alone, except for mountain beavers and deer. Occasionally my friends George Meyer and Malcolm Peterson would share these woods or shore walks. More often solo, I probed old deer runs and Indian trails without ever feeling alone. Here I was at home and at peace – without time restraints except for those marked by seasonal flowers or ripening fruit.

Such delicious freedom of waking up on summer holidays to ask, "What will I do today?" With nostalgia I recalled these easy days when I later read Evelyn Waugh's summing up in *Brideshead Revisited*. Upon reaching middle age he found his emotions little changed from earlier years. He still experienced new enthusiasms and disappointments, fell in and out of love, quickened to a change of place or seasons, and was, in short, the young man he had been – except for time. Now he was so aware of the passing of time he could hardly remember the idle, timeless languor of youth.

SHE GAVE ME THE WORLD

Although I had many aunts and uncles, cousins, and four living grandparents, I was not particularly close to any of them. Instead, I chose and was chosen by two sets of fairy godparents. The first, Marguerite and Myron Murphy, lived across the alley from us when we moved to Northeast 20th Street. The Murphys were both older than my parents and relatively affluent, partly because Marguerite (Peggy) had a career in downtown Seattle at a time when two-income families were rare. They were childless, who knows if by choice. In any case, I loved and was loved by each of them. A tall, gregarious Irishman, Myron was as eager for body contact as I. I rode on his shoulders, sat on his lap for book reading, and some days drove to work with him.

Peggy was stylish, with carefully marcelled auburn hair, lacquered nails, and a distinct scent. She brought home in her ancient touring car intriguing books and masses of cut flowers. Peggy made out that my appearing at her doorstep was a great favor. Sometimes she would send her Airedale terrier, Muggins, with me to the store to bring home a few groceries, including treats for both bearers. Soon I was central to a close relationship between the Murphys and my parents. Saturdays we golfed and on Sundays took long drives together or visited model homes.

We spent my fifth Christmas with their family in Portland, where I suddenly had new, doting grandparents. As usual, Peggy was generous with gifts of big books, Erector Sets, a model train. But best of all was the succession of a desktop globe, an atlas, and then a large world map and a stamp album followed by monthly envelopes of stamps to sort out. I soon learned the countries of each continent, the oceans between, the highest mountains, and the largest rivers. Only average in English and math, I became prodigious in geography and history. The Murphys' extended love gave me confidence; Peggy gave me the world.

Before first grade was over we moved to Bremerton, where Dad was building a waterfront house for Phil and Doris Meyer. Their son George was exactly my age and our two families were close throughout my school and scouting years. The Meyers were also a bit older than my folks and considerably established. Their focusing on George as the perfect boy was fine by me, as I shared their opinion. And besides, their attentions washed over onto George's friend Jack. While my folks tended to do things together, the Meyers planned picnics and fishing outings tailored to the boys' level. Mabel and Elmer avoided the role of parental chauffeurs; George and I were usually taken or picked up by both Doris and Phil.

Phil Meyer, a grocer, landlord, and president of the Lions Club, was a hail-fellow-well-met. A modest person, he took interest in the activities of others, including mine. Doris Meyer had style, a fascination for things visual, a flair for food presentation, and a keen interest in new ideas. I was never so happy as

In my second year of college I became friends with two extraordinary classmates. Both were older and with experiences far beyond campus life. One was a princely Chinese Peruvian, Chan Khan, the other, Ted Herried (right), a tall interior designer who came back for classes with Hope Foote. Ted's openness to all of life and his infatuation with modern and primitive art and with new forms of music and dance considerably widened my horizons. Without success, I attempted to imitate his joie de vivre and his winsome combination of aristocratic nonchalance and old-shoe availability.

at the Meyer house, or so pleased as when I could bicycle out to help George with Saturday chores. Better yet were our frequent weekends together.

Lavished with all this support, George was so content as to resist the new. When he finally learned to swim at eight, I could already log a mile. So it was all through school. I joined Cub Scouts, Boy Scouts, dance class, college *first*. Then George would follow, soon to be my leader. As the Meyers showed particular interest in my design studies and early career, they were often in my thoughts as a young professional. With them in mind, I tried to fortify my parents with proven achievements when friends boasted of new grandchildren.

WEAVING/CALIFORNIA

By my fourth semester at the university my career sights were settled not on architecture, but on interior design. I spent three mornings a week in the furniture design studio and afternoons on junior-year interior projects. With Pat Keller (then Shively), I took Professor Grace Denny's course on textiles: a thorough Home Economics grounding in fibers, structures, and finishes, plus testing, use, and care. I enjoyed learning a universe of terms and names for a hundred cloths. Compared with fine art or even interior styles, this was hard, classifiable information. The time we looked forward to was our turn at a brief stint in the weaving studio "just to better understand how cloth is made." Pat, who knew the famous Dorothy Wright Liebes weave studio in San Francisco, was especially keen on what we could accomplish at a first go. Perhaps she could; I could not. I was slower to learn than any student I have ever taught.

For that first warp I chose a rustic linen that continually broke. In spite of this the teachers encouraged me, perhaps because my approach to color and yarns was unusual or because a man was a rare sight in their studio. I was urged to try again on my own time, and by late spring I was there every available hour. The results became better and more original as I learned coordination and rhythm. Using my hands so much reminded me of Boy Scout handcraft projects I had reveled in.

I also responded positively to the underlying logic of weaving: for every effect, good and bad, a cause could be found. After two years on the drawing board – working not with the materials of architecture, but with pencil and paper to represent something never to be built – making real cloth with actual materials felt good indeed. Woven cloth was also like architecture in being a structure of horizontal and vertical elements dependent for character on the nature of materials, amplified by highlight and shadow. When I gained a little skill I explored some simple patterns, but mostly tried every yarn available, then wove with straw, bamboo, raffia, wire, rope, and rags. Every strand of nature, it seemed, could be woven. So could the look and feel of it, as I tried weaving to express the furrowed rows of planted fields. When I read that Vincent van Gogh had developed color breakthroughs by manipulating dyed yarns, I wove what I thought to be the chromatic expressions of Japan and India. After seeing an exhibition by the pioneer Abstract Expressionist Clyfford Still, I worked all night attempting to capture the emotion I felt in his burning, saturated play of color.

Just as I was learning to weave I became close friends with a princely Peruvian architecture student, Chan Khan. Chan, the last direct male descendant of Kublai Khan, was born in Lima as the son of the Chinese ambassador. Because his father had donated large parks in Lima, experimental farms to the nation, and finally their home to be the vice-presidential palace, Chan inherited the right to export antiquities. He was bringing to Seattle Pre-Columbian fabric collections that would become the chief textile holdings of America's great museums. While these magnificent textiles were being restored and mounted, I had free access to examine them, to learn from their amazing constructions and the heady color systems of Paracas embroidered mantles and needleknit bands.

I was completing work with Grace Denny on her pivotal translation of Raoul D'Harcourt's *The Textiles of Ancient Peru and Their Techniques,* which would become a bible for both weavers and anthropologists. My assignment to describe very complex textile structures often required making at least diagrammatic reconstructions. In learning perforce and firsthand the "bone structures" of extremely advanced cloths, sometimes four-layered, I became quite familiar with the principles of fabric structure. As Professor Denny, in consultation with Dr. Weibel and Irene Emory, was developing an analysis of all fabric structures, I was exposed to those principles of classification that have guided me ever since.

Classification probably sounds like a dry concept, but it is not. Rather, it provides a skeleton on which to hang all other information. In making classifications, one also learns that one such system of order reveals a universe filled with parallel systems: there is a sensible logic to all we ever know. Somehow,

After her retirement as Professor of Interior Architecture, Hope Foote accepted a post at Southern Illinois University at Carbondale, where Buckminster Fuller and other great minds combatted backwater regionalism and rural poverty. Built for combat, she was a wise choice. She immediately attacked the prevailing small-mindedness by goading the youngest elements into revolt. I was one of those she called down for reinforcement. Did she ever understand that one of the reasons I became a weaver was my reluctance to finish her senior design class?

too, in this experience there was a connection to the logic and metaphysics that I studied with open-mouthed enthusiasm in the graduate seminars in cultural anthropology, and even to the sensual magic of color reducible to the most comprehensible of systems.

A new idea was forming. Perhaps instead of becoming an interior architect, I could be a weaver. I thought about this throughout an engaging, meaningful summer job working with underprivileged junior high school students. They were not particularly poor, but without parents who could take them outside their neighborhood. Soon I had the boys going on camping trips and museum visits, and to night baseball games, the national crew races, and swimming meets. My right hand in all of this was Tommy, an undersized redhead who had been the first to arrive. Busy with laying out art supplies, I asked him to be responsible for the sports equipment. He took charge like a general, becoming my faithful attaché all through the summer. I learned only later that the year before Tommy had thrown rocks through four hundred school windows.

Finishing this program several weeks before the university resumed, I headed off alone to San Francisco. Like other visitors there, I was much taken by the seven hills and all the mysteries in between. Too soon a severe chest pain prompted a doctor's visit with a diagnosis of three broken ribs and a prescription to go rest on a beach. I checked Le Corbusier's books on architecture out of the library and headed toward Carmel. I'd never seen country so beautiful as the rolling, golden hills punctuated with ancient live oak trees and the rich, purple-black furrows of artichokes near Salinas. In Monterey I rented a turret on top of a gingerbread mansion. From there I took grapes, jack cheese, and a book to hitch a ride through the famous Seventeen-Mile Drive to Carmel. This was made easier by visitors thinking they had found a local artist.

One day I walked to the top of Jack's Peak to see a famous modern house by Richard Neutra. Finding no one at home, I pressed my nose to the windows. On the way back I was picked up by the Blair sisters, two beauties with a pottery studio on Fishermen's Wharf in Monterey and the largest Buick convertible. They knew Mary Blinks, who owned the house, and said they would ask for a dinner invitation. Mary happily obliged by inviting us and pointed out all the good and bad features of this noble house, then showed us the few other modern landmarks. In New York five years later, I watched a heavyset woman in a rain slicker lumbering up the stairs to my studio. It was Mary, by then a weaver making pilgrimages to well-known weave studios. She did not remember my name but was pleased to find a familiar face. Before her recent death at about one hundred she had become something of a historian on weavers and their considerable patron.

Through the Blairs I met the manager of Gump's Carmel, who offered me a job on the sales floor. I took it, as well as the Blairs' offer to stay at their house, which was within walking distance. At their Labor Day house party I met two young men from Los Angeles, one a dentist, the other Robert Graham Chase, who had gone on from Dartmouth to study architecture under Mies van der Rohe and then to study ballet under Madame Nijinska. After a few days together at Big Sur and moonlit nights listening to Debussy, they asked me to motor back down the coast with them. Why not? I had already determined that Southern Californians were sufficiently uninhibited as to have a special style.

In Los Angeles they showed me only the good parts of the city: Sunset Drive, Beverly Hills and Bel Air, and the beach at Malibu. I met Dorothea Hulse, who owned Handcraft House, a handweaving studio that functioned as both a "school to the stars" and a custom weave shop. Dorothea, who had woven "the Robe" for the popular biblical film, asked if I would consider teaching modern color and design in exchange for lessons in what I did not know. When Bob Chase, who lived at Lafayette Park near her studio, said I could stay with him for a while, I went home to Seattle to break the news. It was not well received. While even interior architecture sounded like a respectable profession, being a weaver did not. Dropping out of school, even for a while, was unacceptable. If I persisted, all funds would be cut off. I left without a blessing, but with a full food hamper for the long trip south.

Dorothea Hulse was a compassionate surrogate mother. Through her I wove for Mary Martin and taught directors' wives and stars like Joan Crawford, who wanted to weave dress material for the little daughter who would later write *Mommie Dearest*. I met Lavonne Carlson, a designer with the Viennese architect Victor Gruen, and took part in that studio's familial parties. Through Madame Nijinska I enjoyed the company of other fun-loving European émigrés. Life seemed like a bowl of cherries, even if I could not afford any.

To earn pocket money I scraped candle wax from the Rococo torchères of a rich young man hosting grand soirées with the hope of acting in movies. For seemingly grand sums I occasionally worked as an extra in Western films. In November I took a Christmas job at nearby Bullock's Wilshire, at that time the world's most spectacular store. After half a day in giftwrap, I was selected to assist the manager of the Futures Department across the street, which meant stashing away large gifts for holiday delivery at a specific hour. This was great, because as soon as I finished the day's assignment I could skip back to Handcraft House, just two blocks away. On occasional visits to the University of Southern California library, I felt college students were privileged in being allowed to learn full-time.

When I was home at Christmas, Dad was sufficiently mollified that I would enroll in USC's School of Architecture to pay that Harvard-sized tuition, but he would send no allowance to Southern California. Near the campus I shared a house with two graduate students. The best parts of this arrangement were that one of them liked to cook and that I could pick lemons from a tree outside my bedroom window. I bought a used bicycle, studied philosophy and French, and took a seminar in modern art with visits to the outstanding collections of Vincent Price and Edward G. Robinson.

The philosophy classes were eye-openers. Logic stimulated my intellect, as did the arguments of the neo-Platonists and the metaphysical search for the "really real." The concept of a direct relationship between truth and beauty emanating from the same force appealed to me. So did the elegance of economy and, at that time, asceticism.

At the same time, I marveled at the ranges of texture in California foliage and the remarkable cones and seed pods I collected on bike rides. Some of these I tried to weave into long strips of samples made on a loom at home. When Dorothy Liebes invited me for a trunk showing, I brought these along. Laying them across a bed, she said, "What wonderful stripes! It would be good to have you spend time in the studio, but you are an innovator, and in my studio there is only one designer."

After summer quarter at USC, my folks paid a visit with the proposition that if I would come back to Seattle, they would release money from my grandfather. I could be independent and receive for my twenty-first birthday a fine new loom. We drove up the coast together, stopping to see my friends in Carmel.

On Sundays Lavonne Carlson and I drove her roadster out to the mile-long wild beach at Malibu. Now it's hard to remember when sun, sand, and surf seemed sufficient diversion for whole days on end.

Out of hundreds of portraits, I have two favorites, taken about twenty years apart by two friends: the first one, on page 6, is by Olga Gueft; and this one is by Dorothy Beskind.

Back at the university in Seattle I was allowed a special course focusing on fabric design. I spent spare time making useful fabrics, mostly upholsteries and blinds to go into Northwest houses. I experimented, seeking skill and expression for all those pent-up feelings of the unvocal young. I wanted to excel and to be needed. While still searching, I would try to project through teaching the certainty of my jerry-built philosophy. This opportunity came when Ed Rossbach came from Cranbrook Academy of Art to teach weaving for the art department and asked if I would be his graduate assistant. I had never taken an eight o'clock class and teaching one was not easy. Otherwise, this three-term relationship was pivotal in my learning experience. Rossbach's approach to teaching was so highly disciplined as to be foolproof. Students wove a series of samples of basic weaves using sturdy plied wool yarns dyed in bold colors. While I was explaining techniques and Rossbach's reasons behind them, he wove experimentally. As I rather enjoyed being part of the teaching staff, I considered what it would be like to be a professor. Perhaps I could teach weaving until I had a doctorate and could lecture on philosophy. Ed encouraged me to think about the master's degree program at Cranbrook, then recommended me for a scholarship there.

Another opportunity came when the Seattle Weavers Guild asked Rossbach to teach a two-week intensive course at the Seattle Art Museum and he declined in my favor. Forty

A lifelong friendship with Elizabeth Bayley Willis has enriched my mind and spirit. It was Betty who opened my eyes to the richness and diversity of Asian fabrics when I was still an undergraduate.

With my longtime friends and clients Patricia and Dale Keller at the opening of my exhibition at the Palais du Louvre in Paris, 1981.

Win Anderson, president of Larsen Design Studio, was my longtime sounding board and traveling companion. I relied on her common sense and ingenuity in problem solving.

women brought small looms to the museum to weave through my exercises in the joy of developing rich textures and iridescent color. This proved so popular that I was soon teaching similar groups on an ongoing basis, for what seemed like handsome fees.

All these things I did from an artist's studio building near the campus. On the lobby directory "Jack Larsen, Weaver" attracted a housewife carrying her husband's torn pants for mending. This slight was rare; it was in Seattle that I gained sufficient encouragement and the confidence to realign my sights. The time frame helped, particularly in the ten postwar years when changes came so quickly, when Beaux-Arts architecture caved in to modernism, and when the Northwest houses individually designed and furnished by our regional architects demanded new cloths unavailable from commercial fabric manufacturers. To express the materials and structure of their making, their place and function called for custom-designed, handwoven cloths. This was an easy market to enter. With handlooms and the availability of many yarn types in every color, and with the acquaintance of the leading young architects, commissions came as quickly as they could be woven. Out of this small success rose the question of what might lie beyond, what other opportunities might open up.

Marianne Strengell, my weavemaster at Cranbrook, was, at midcentury, one of our most influential fabric designers. Best known for her plays of texture in a somber Finnish palette, she was upset with what she termed my "California colors."

Opposite: The thirteen consecutive years I taught at Haystack Mountain School of Crafts in Maine were a spectacular respite from the city, with some time to weave new cloths in sunlight on the weave deck. I am proud of having selected Edward Larrabee Barnes for the Deer Isle campus, still new in this 1963 photograph.

CRANBROOK

To reach Cranbrook I boarded a Pullman car speeding across the desolate plains of Montana and the Dakotas into the greenery surrounding the Great Lakes and Chicago. My first pilgrimages were to Louis Sullivan's architecture, Mies van der Rohe's campus for Armour Institute, and the Impressionist masterpieces at the Art Institute. From Sullivan's old South Station, the grand trunk railroad carried me to Detroit, then a cab took me on a long ride out Woodward Avenue to Lone Pine Road and onto a dream campus. In those days Cranbrook Academy of Art still maintained the aura of an ivory tower where sixty-five graduate students were comforted, their number matched by sixty-five gardeners working hundreds of acres. Eliel Saarinen's well-crafted architecture and Carl Milles's sculpture punctuated the huge campus, surrounded by verdant estates. The countryside was also beautiful, with dominant eastern hardwood trees coloring gloriously in autumn. Even the tall prairie grasses took on such splendid shades of aubergine that I was tempted to weave them! The annual rummage sale at Cranbrook's Christ Church Cathedral provided not only warm winter clothes, but also insights into another lifestyle of bespoke garments made by the great tailors of Europe.

My room in the new men's dormitory (overlooking Milles's Jonah Pool, where we could still swim) was more than adequate. So was my huge loom in Loja Saarinen's former studio. Classmates were congenial, especially Joy Lind, the tall Detroit weaver who was an old hand at Cranbrook. Side by side, she and I knotted huge Swedish-style *flossa* rugs for weeks on end and designed together a warp to be woven on the power loom. As students, we didn't see weavemaster Marianne Strengell very much; mostly we watched her briskly walk past to her own studio adjoining ours. House rules were that our studio was to be dark at 11:30 P.M. and not reopened until 7. Most of us read this to mean we would be there all those long, productive hours.

Six weeks into the semester, Marianne called me into her studio to say she was disappointed in my production. To my defense that I was outperforming the others, she explained that as I was the scholarship student she expected double the quantity as well as quality of the others. Thus I learned how to work at a breakneck pace that would serve me well in the start-up years of my company and to become sufficiently organized to be

In 1972 I showed the blossom colors of my new Thai Silk Collection to my friend, the interior designer Andrée Putman, the doyenne of French taste. She responded, "Jacques, don't you know that color is *over*?"

Mother at the opening of our Los Angeles showroom with our longtime vice president, Bob Carr. Our Wilton carpet behind them is Happiness.

offered a degree show in one year. Over Christmas break on the West Coast I did research for my thesis at handweaving studios from Seattle to Los Angeles, and sent back five-inch-wide redwood fencing to weave into a massive screen, now in a Montreal museum.

Having finished my large commission for Roland Terry's Smith House in Seattle, I spent the long winter semester with Win Anderson, my fellow student and future business associate, concentrating on fabric printing. During long months of snow cover, I learned how to wind a wide warp for a three-yard exhibition piece, thread it, and weave it down in a single day. While weaving I would plan the next project, and calculate in my head the amount of yarn needed. In school I had never excelled at arithmetic, but now that numbers had meaning, I could readily deal with them. At a lecture I challenged Minoru Yamasaki's selection of Barcelona chairs for the lobby of the library at

As chair of the American jury for the Fashion Foundation's International Textile Design Contest in 1988, I stand between Yoshiko Wada, Maria Tulokas, Mary McFadden, and Mildred Constantine (Bill Blass is missing). Since winning, at five, a prize in a Metropolitan Life drawing contest, I have been keen on competitions.

My friend and guru Ingeborg Ten Haeff once told a mutual acquaintance, "You feel that as friends of Jack's we have something in common; the big difference is you learn from Jack, and Jack learns from me." Ingeborg also once told me, "Don't put flowers in that, it looks like a vase!"

My best English friend, Audrey Levy, joined me in Tokyo for a Fashion Foundation International jury. With her I share passions such as textiles, teaching, and all aspects of gardening.

Wayne State University. Thirty years later I would remind him of this when he became the best client for Larsen Furniture! As a new friend of the great art collector Lydia Winston, the daughter of architect Albert Kahn, I wove upholsteries and draperies for her Birmingham house. The concentrated productivity in my Cranbrook days was occasionally broken by Carl Milles's parties and by lectures at the Detroit Institute of Art, including one where I met Anni and Josef Albers.

Following publication of Gertrude Greer's *Adventures in Weaving*, for which I had woven the illustrations, I was visited by editors and invited to lecture at museums in Indianapolis and Columbus. I drove off with a car full of potters to the Syracuse Ceramic National Exhibition, where Peter Voulkos first exhibited. Over spring break I drove with classmates to New York City, which I found so exciting that I seldom slept. An introduction to the print designer Don Wight led to insights into the textile design world and the pleasures of a great city. By day I showed my portfolio to dozens of design houses. In an early heat wave, wearing a new summer suit, I mustered up courage to call on everyone I could think of. The Cranbrook connection opened doors and everyone was kind. Florence Knoll was encouraging but found my style too individual for her focus. My big chance came with Lydia Winston's introduction to

A sunny spring day on the wall of a tulip-filled garden at Round House.

Herbert Rothschild, who owned several modern furniture companies. He greeted me warmly and, with his top staff, carefully appraised my portfolio and then went into a huddle. The verdict was, "We not only doubt that your designs can be produced, but know they won't sell on the American market." Somehow I doubted their judgment. Thirty years later a letter arrived from Rothschild, who had not forgotten that first meeting. He wrote, "I've made many mistakes in my life but have not usually been that far off base. I'm happy to have been wrong, and to have lived all these years with your fabrics."

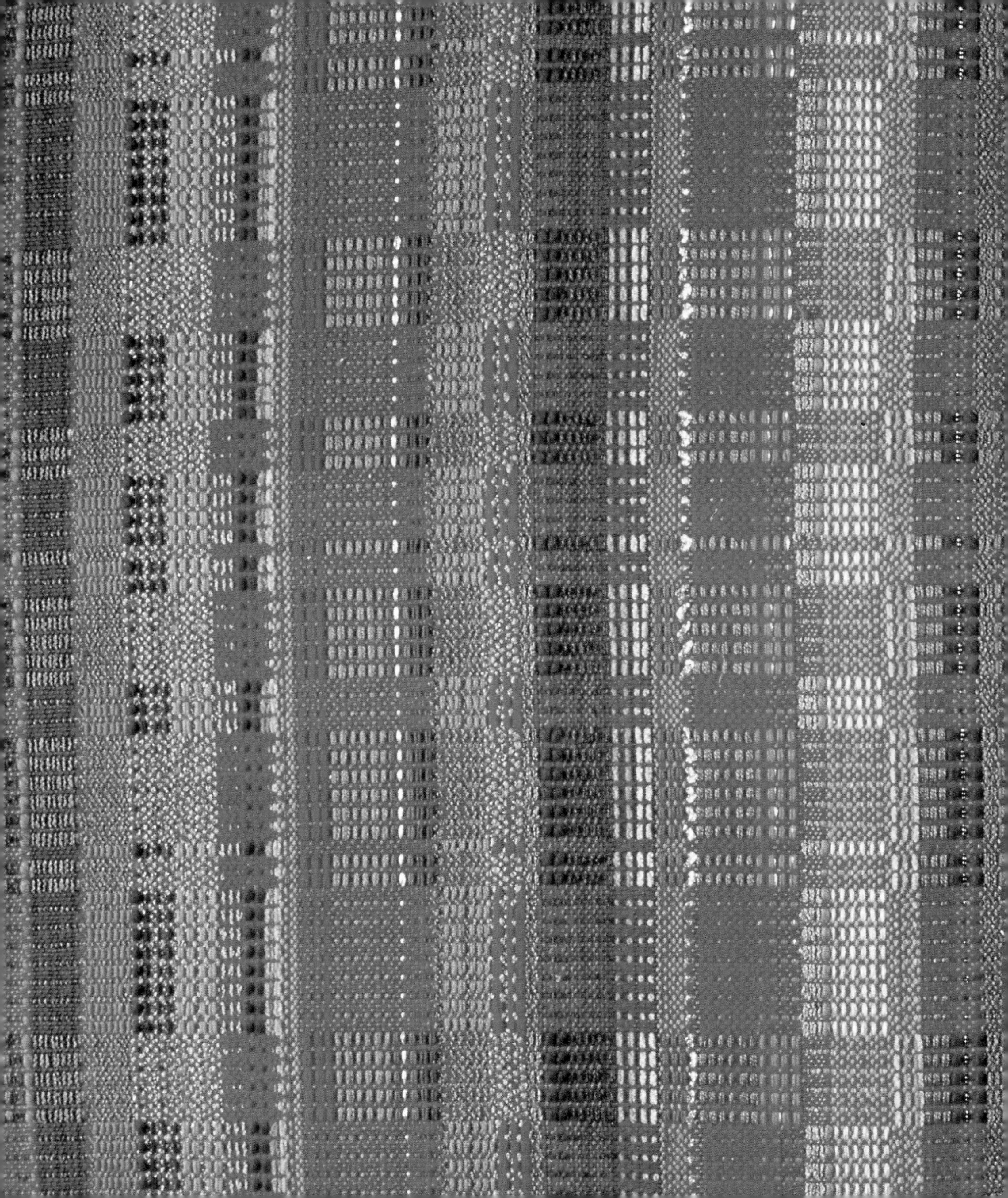

STARTING UP Cranbrook degree shows and graduation over in June of 1951,

I traveled west with the thought of writing a book on modern fabric design

while deciding my future. I stopped with a friend in Mill Valley until summer

CHAPTER 2

Design

fog and dripping eucalyptus trees became too depressing. I rented a studio

in San Francisco's Flatiron Building but, before moving, decided to go back to

Seattle for the summer. I had never thought of Seattle as sunny but, compared

to the Bay Area, at least it had a summer. Once there, a designer friend asked if

I would weave some decorative pillows, then suggested I offer them to a San

Francisco showroom. As I had the yarns and my friend Win Anderson the

looms, it was easy to weave pillow fabrics more glamorous than anyone would

want for larger areas. They sold well.

"Be an open bowl, that some opportunity might fall in."
— A Chinese proverb carved on a stone lintel at the Henry Art Gallery, Seattle

Left: A slubby white linen with randomly spaced warp and weft, Mondrian was one of our first casement cloths. It was originally produced as a shirting for Mark Cross. This sheer version, with a weft of pearlescent slit film yarn, we named Montego.

Right: I designed Jason as a diaphanous veil to separate the unpolished white marble entertaining areas of Eero Saarinen's Irwin Miller house. Openings in the randomly spaced warp caused the goat hair and gimp wefts to loop and curl above the fabric surface.

 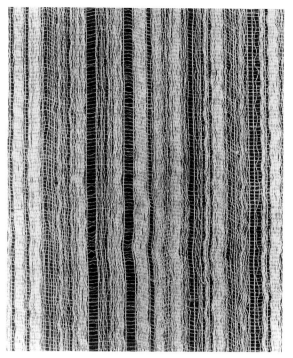

Previous spread: Remulade, from our Spice Garden Collection of 1954, began at Haystack as a hanging woven with perhaps one hundred wefts. When clients wanted to order it for upholstery, I turned it ninety degrees and reduced the yarns to a few dozen that could be reordered. Then we learned to powerweave it with three warp beams and a number of weighted spools hanging off the back of the loom.

Job offers came via Cranbrook. Would I teach at the University of Illinois? Or would I come to the Saarinen-designed art center in Des Moines, where I would have a fine studio and teach only three days a week? Then I heard from New York. Thaibok Fabrics asked if I would design an American collection for them; Arundell Clarke, the English-born fabric innovator who had started up Knoll Textiles, suggested working with him on a freelance basis. While the teaching offers were quite secure, my thinking was that if I could move three looms and thirty-nine cases of yarn to the Midwest, I could also send them to New York, the first place where I had felt at home. And so I did, slow freight, collect. As this could take four weeks, I decided to go east by train, stopping in San Francisco. There, a friendly voice on the telephone called out, "Dorothy, Jack Larsen is here!" It was Harry Lawenda, the sales agent who had taken my pillows. And soon I was adopted by the Lawendas. Wouldn't I show with the Bauhaus potter Marguerite Wildenhain at the Pacifica exhibition? For this same huge California design exhibit, wouldn't I stay to weave a glorious fabric for Lawenda's new sofa design, to be on the cover of *House & Garden*?

During the day I wove in Mary Walker Phillips's studio, other times I was shown the insider's Bay Area: over to Oakland to meet Dorothy's pal Trader Vic; to Orinda to dine with the design impresario Barbara Dorn; out with Peter Rooke-Ley and Bill Brewer, who with the Lawendas would soon recycle the historic district of Jackson Square as America's first design center. Although I enjoyed the whirlwind, it so drained my resources that I cashed in the New York train ticket to board an eastbound Greyhound.

Upon arrival in New York I received a letter from Eleanor Lloyd Richards, asking if I would call on her. Remembering the Cranbrook legend that she had requested an opportunity to teach weavers how to spin wool, then arrived with a chauffeur in a car too long for the garage *and* a flock of sheep – I called. A pleasant lunch discussion of our shared enthusiasm for weaving and of my nebulous plans to create a New York studio resulted in a check large enough to pay for the looms and yarns arriving from Seattle. Scion of one of Manhattan's old Dutch families, Mrs. Richards was helping weavers in war-torn Europe and Japan – and here, as well. She was a patron of Mary Hambidge's Rabun Studio shop, which sold extraordinary tweeds spun and woven in rural Georgia. Through her, I met Mrs. Hambidge, as well as the furniture maker George Nakashima, who showed at Rabun Studio.

Mrs. Richards entertained my occasional guests at her East Side townhouse and in her Japanese garden at Rye. In her long car we motored out to craftsmen's studios she found special. When I gave my first party, she sent her driver and cook over with dinner. The elderly editor of *Handweaver & Craftsman* was similarly helpful in introducing me to the few other weavers and yarn dealers in the area and in commissioning occasional essays. The first of these was to cover the International Textile Design Competition in Greensboro, North Carolina, where the sole juror, architect Alexander Girard, awarded me two prizes.

Arundell Clarke explained that he could not hire my design services because he had just bought a fine house on 73rd Street near Madison Avenue. But, if I would clean up the top floor sufficiently for my studio, I could have it rent-free for the first six months. I would help him with some projects and, if my design was accepted, weave the lobby curtain for Lever House – New York's first International Style office tower. This was not to

For the curtain of the Phoenix Opera House we machine-embroidered yarns in eight "Southwest colors" over mirror Mylar. This produced a lively play of light reflecting on the audience. When I sent a large sample to the fabricator for a dry-cleaning test his response was, "Sonny, each half of that curtain is three hundred yards. If you are lucky, they will vacuum it."

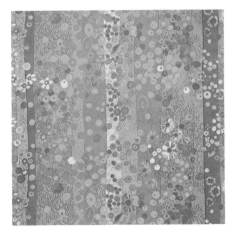

Win and I worked with artist Don Wight for a year to create the complex pattern Primavera, which loosely translated to cloth our passion for the paintings of Gustav Klimt. It took even longer to develop a dense cotton velvet with a pile short enough that we could print through all of it. Although the result startled the design world, at first orders were few because clients were unsure how to use it. When they learned how sensuous and practical it was for upholstery we had difficulty producing enough.

From 1964 to 1984 I worked in a large sky-lighted cube within the Larsen Design Studio. Our color planning originated here, but was finalized – as it is now – in the viewing room under the constancy of the same par-lamp floodlights used in our showrooms. When we know the light source of site-specific installations, color decisions are made in light similar to those conditions.

be a simple window casement, but a ceremonial drapery within the space for which I devised a translucent lace weave of linen cord and gold metal. Clarke's East Side address was prestigious, his two showroom floors were starkly handsome, and his clients worked on cutting-edge projects. My skylighted space was also quite adequate, with four rooms plus a bath so large that it doubled as office space. The four flights proved surmountable to a few of Clarke's clients and to editors in search of the new.

I soon found an assistant, Ginger Marindale, a young Beverly Hills debutante who preferred weaving to college. We both lived and worked like Californians. Efficiency within a relaxed studio atmosphere was easy, as the phone seldom rang and client visits were few. With our Czech apprentice we prepared hearty salads for lunches, which included any friends around. I was happy to see Ginger come in the morning and leave at night. I read voraciously, enjoyed new friends, and felt (for the last time) caught up.

Although my Seattle friend Margaret Hosmer had been stern in her admonition not to wear "Seattle clothes" in New York, I continued to use my own ties handwoven as a heavily textured ribbon shaped on the loom. The manager of a new-wave men's store called Casualaire asked where I had bought my tie. "I wove it," I responded. "How many can you weave before Christmas?" he wanted to know. When we agreed upon a price and advance for seven hundred ties to be woven in three months, I started a cottage industry. Using several yarn types, I wound long warps to be given out with appropriate wefts to handweavers. I would dye the finished ties and make delivery.

These transactions provided income and served as entrée to other buyers. I was commissioned to weave linen shirtings for Mark Cross. Through the menswear designer Alexander Shields I was introduced to the trendy tailor called Lord of New York to weave one-of-a-kind suitings blending exotic fibers. These I scoured in the big bathtub before they were cut to the frames of the international set, including the Duke and Duchess of Windsor (who typically did not pay the tailor). Better yet was meeting such men as Alexander Calder, Leonard Bernstein, I. M. Pei, and Alexander Girard, all wearing my shaggy ties. Most of them did not enjoy neckties, but when forced to, found mine preferable to conventional ones.

My ongoing museum lectures on modern design and color theory for weavers were so successful that I advertised a round-robin correspondence course for handweavers. A New York schoolteacher, Fan Mason, insisted she wanted these lessons one-on-one and would pay double. This began a long friendship. In 1953, when my new company made a stock offering, she badgered her family and weaver-friends into subscribing and thus earned a seat on our small board. Her son David became our accountant, then treasurer. She and two friends also became my most exacting tie weavers!

Manning Field and the friendly crew at Thaibok Ltd. were both encouraging and open-minded in the early days of my company. Thaibok had been started by American Field Service buddies as the North American franchise for Jim Thompson's Siamese Silk Company. By 1951, when their thriving new business seemed threatened by a communist invasion of Thailand, they asked if I would design an American line to augment their silk sales and, if necessary, grow to replace it. My first designs were powerwoven linen upholsteries. When I suggested we could not take them further without talking to their weaving mill, they responded, "Don't *you* know a mill? We do not." Those Clarke knew were too large, but I found Dick Bolan, a fine old Italian weaver, and rented one commercial loom in New Jersey. With Thaibok funding we bought two tons of linen, dyed it, and started production.

The famous furniture designer Edward Wormley commissioned casements for exhibit spaces, then bamboo blinds for Dunbar Furniture showrooms. Marie Phenyo of New Design commissioned an upholstery yardage I laboriously wove while Ginger was on holiday. Thanks to Clarke, young designers from leading firms specializing in banks and offices began to mount the stairs. As their orders were too large to handweave at 73rd Street, Dick Bolan and I learned to powerweave more and more complex assemblages of exotic yarns. Craftsmanship and ingenuity, I soon learned, were not limited to handweaving, nor did they require art-school training.

To simulate – even exaggerate – the irregular spacing of handweaves we learned to weave with one shuttle empty to randomly space out the wefts. Later, to achieve this effect more economically, Bolan filed off occasional teeth of the pick gear that controlled weft spacing. Similarly, we removed teeth (dents)

Edward Wormley's famous Edward Chair, in natural ash and bronze, is as architectonic as it is comfortable. Our pebbly handwoven Tyrol wool cloth seems its perfect cover.

After establishing Larsen International in Zurich, in 1961, we moved our European headquarters to Germany to be inside the Common Market. Here is Larsen Haus in Stuttgart, in the late seventies. With a bank on the street floor, we occupied a slim tower only eight stories above ground, but the tallest building on King's Park.

from the comblike reed that controlled vertical spacing of the warp. By doing this we could eventually weave with strips of leather or braid up to half an inch in width. I would present the challenge, sometimes with a clue toward resolution. Bolan would "sleep on it," dream of a solution, and rush down to the mill at three in the morning to "check it out." Most often he would then call and ask Ginger to meet him at the George Washington Bridge to pick up the sample.

This process was simple, fast, and as cost-effective as real teamwork can be. Mill people always referred to what we did as "handweaving." They found our yards-per-shift ratio lamentable but, in a way, it was handcraft on power looms. We maintained direct control, flexibility, and quality: because we bought the yarns, there was no temptation at mill level to adulterate quality. The custom orders had another advantage. There was almost always an overage from which we could cut display lengths and samples. Soon Harry and Dorothy Lawenda of Kneedler-Fauchere were representing our new company in California; Barbara Dorn launched one of the first of our tiny collections in her Miami showroom. At Dorn's insistence, I learned something about the color effect of tropical light. Even after I lightened a palette she dubbed "Scandinavian," my fabrics looked oppressively heavy there. She persisted, I learned, and in so doing changed the color range of our collections.

As the yarns for my heavily textured fabrics were primarily dull cottons, linens, and jute, colorings loaded with yellow dye seemed the most vibrant. Olives, ochers, caramel, and earthy oranges could be used at full intensity without seeming aggressive. These shades also worked well with oiled wood finishes and complemented the sharp blue-greens then popular. Eventually our evolving palette was so popular that Florence Knoll adopted it to replace the primary red, yellow, and blue that had been a Knoll trademark. Eventually, too, my olives and ochers were popularized to become the saccharin Avocado and Harvest Gold color epidemic of the American sixties. At Larsen Design Studio we changed color directions – slowly. Acceptance of the new (and rejection of the familiar) took longer then, before color printing in design magazines was common, and before Middle America was on the same wavelength as New York and California. With a certain nostalgia I recall the time when the same two colorings towered at the top of our sales chart for a decade. No longer!

Probably the most complex terry cloth ever woven, this is a jacquard-woven towel we made for J. P. Stevens in the late 1960s, when our first carpet designs suggested similar techniques. The Architecture pattern uses two shaded warp stripes with various "tweeds" combining the two. The bas-relief in its several forms derives from voided velvet techniques.

A heavy slub-spun worsted is plain woven for a durable upholstery with the luster of silk. Here is Cashel, from the Irish Awakening Collection, 1969.

Barbara Dorn soon threw us another challenge. On a trip to Haiti she met a French painter who had noticed locals rolling wild magnolia fiber against their thighs to spin wicking for tin-can oil lamps. "This," he told them "is yarn. If you can make yarn, you can also weave!" He brought in some looms and they began weaving. Barbara's request was that I work with these new weavers, find fast dyestuffs for them, and distribute their cloths. In short order I was able to dispatch a DuPont dye team to Haiti. They somehow achieved colorfastness with kettle-in-the-yard conditions, even in the Haitians' unique resist method of winding yarn into a tight ball, then dyeing it to achieve a random dark-and-light pattern. I added twills and then brocading to their weaving capability, designed bold stripes, and soon found a considerable market for these cloths and rugs.

As important as the commercial success, our year-old operation was now importing and, for the first time, working in the Third World. Equally significant, I had learned the simple beauty inherent in handwoven cloths made with yarns handspun of ungraded fiber. Their organic variations in texture and color became the perfect antidote for monotonous surfaces of laminate and drywall soon dominating interior spaces. I came to the conclusion that the great loss of the Industrial Revolution was not handweaving, but handspinning. Our success in this venture would lead us to influential clients such as Marcel Breuer and invitations to work with handspinning operations in Morocco and Mexico, and then to the masterful Colombian handspinners and weavers whom we still engage for the Doria range.

In one year things had come a long way. We were launched in New York with powerweaving and were now developing design for import as well. Prizes and exhibitions were almost as useful as the generous press notices given this newcomer. Only finance was troublesome. Because growth required capital that was noticeably absent, my thought was, "I still may starve, but at least there will be an obituary."

In 1952, at the end of my first summer, I was approached to buy (at five cents on the dollar) a defunct handweaving studio on 22nd Street near Park Avenue South. Eleanor Richards loaned me the money to acquire the heavy dobby looms and a warping mill, automatic bobbin winders, and a considerable stock of yarn – all in an affordable space, with trained dobby-loom weavers! This turned out to be a giant step. Business was soon so brisk I was running two shifts, then designing at midnight. I built a shipping table and – too often – was asleep on it when the first weavers arrived in the morning. As the first janitor and first shipping clerk, I learned how to train my replacements.

Help arrived when a divorced socialite, Marian Mitchell, took over the office. Win Anderson came on from Cranbrook to be the first production manager, soon replaced by a weaver from Los Angeles, Bob Carr. Then Win became associate designer, as we customized dozens of fabrics and blinds each month. We attempted to employ handicapped weavers but failed, not because of their physical disabilities, but because the ones we hired had psychological problems. Instead, we became a magnet for artists coming out of Cranbrook and Black Mountain College. These young people were so flexible as to soon learn simple weaving or the office skills required. Like craftsmen, they readily identified problems, then resolved them. One fall day most of the weavers did not show up, nor did they call. It was Yom Kippur, which I did not know about; nor did I know most of the staff were Jewish!

We incorporated that second fall (1952) with a small infusion of capital and a promise of more from our accountants. When more money was not forthcoming, Marian discovered that the fine print in our agreement with the accountants stated they each had 25 percent of the shares. The squabble ended when our scrappy North Carolina lawyer threatened them with bankruptcy. "For a designer," he explained, "this would not be serious but, for accountants, a lifelong blemish." Thus confronted, the bullies meekly retreated. David Mason came on as our after-hours accountant. We reincorporated in early 1953 with a unique stock offer protecting shareholders with keyman insurance, preferred shares, and preemptive rights. Most of those who bought a few shares did so with the feeling that Jack needed the money more than the Red Cross. These shares became valuable only in the sixties.

For many years sales grew and, with them, overheads and inventories, but not the bottom line. Early discussions of a merger with Thaibok Fabric had been attractive to me because they were a friendly team when I seemed pretty much alone. As Thaibok was cash rich and I had only potential, terms could not be fixed. Instead, I built my own group, which soon included the key players from Thaibok. Chief among them was the company's former president, Manning Field. Manning was first our business manager and then, until his retirement, company philosopher and leader of the opposition: the only real mistakes we made were on the rare occasions when Manning and I agreed on some wrong direction.

Derived from Celtic scrollwork, Oberon is the only fabric in the Irish Awakening Collection not woven in Ireland. The sheer voile areas between the volutes were printed with acid to dissolve the cotton fiber – a process called *devore*.

At age thirty-four I experienced some changes. I had moved to the parlor floor at 27 West 9th Street, with space for personal entertaining and something of a home life. As our company was growing and paying dividends to shareholders, it occurred to me that perhaps I was not just playing hard, but actually working. I had always said I would never work. It also occurred to me that, if I could do this one thing successfully, perhaps I could succeed in difficult personal areas. I started eleven years of intensive analysis, five hours a week. First it became apparent that my psyche had not grown much since the day, at age nineteen, I decided to single-mindedly focus on career activities. Next came the discovery that I would not have taken that decision at nineteen except for having the personality of an eleven-year-old! Next, things improved.

CLIENTS AND COMMISSIONS

As I recall, my first client while still back in Seattle was Bill Teeters, my deskmate in junior year who was heir to Delteet, the largest modern furniture store north of San Francisco. Even when I was just beginning to weave, he would modestly ask me to produce a small custom yardage. What I remember most was my consternation in being as pleased by the tangible approval of being paid for my work as by the creation of the design.

My first "big" client was Arthur Morgan, who spoke to our design class when he came to Seattle to found the office of industrial designer Walter Darwin Teague at Boeing. When I told him that I was a weaver, he asked to stop by my studio. He wanted to come by really early, on his way to work. Although very much a night person, I accepted a 7:00 A.M. date. In my tiny studio all was in readiness – the samples, the best coffee bowls, some fruit and flowers – before I crawled into my unusual bed, a large drawer that pulled out from under the raised dressing-room floor. The next thing I knew, the studio door opened in the dark, and something very large fell on me. It was Mr. Morgan; I had slept through my alarm! Somehow we both got up and closed the oversize drawer. I found some clothes and Mr. Morgan left me a small order for his wife's birthday. When later he opened his own interior design office we became good friends. After I moved to New York, he was my muse as I started a decades-long series of personalized form letters to clients; I called this my "Dear Arthur" list.

Soon after I had moved to a larger studio in the Kennedy Building, I was called on by my former professor Hope Foote. She was redoing the Allen House in the Highlands for the Boeing president and she needed several textured natural upholsteries. From my stack of mounted samples she found two that would do, "if only they could be ever so slightly deeper but cleaner, the color of well-cooked wild duck – cool with warm shadows." I immediately set to work on more samples. After these failed to satisfy, as did those prepared for the third visit, I brought out my two original samples. Suddenly her eyes lit up. "Oh Jack," she purred while writing the deposit check, "I know how hard you have worked on this, but how your taste has improved in the process!"

My classmate and friend Chan Khan, who had first met Roland Terry in Lima, convinced this Seattle architect to consider me a source for his projects. First I wove a small commission for him, then a substantial order for lush bamboo blinds on the lake-facing window walls of the Smith House. This was the beginning of a decades-long relationship, as Roland expanded his clientele to become the dominant architect working in the Northwest Style. When our accounting department pressed for payment on our fabrics for his Hilton Inn in Seattle he wrote, "You are the best fabric designer, but not the only one. Why not be a little patient as my office and the builders have to be?" He rewarded our ensuing patience with substantial orders for some fine restaurants and Nordstrom's first and flagship store in Seattle.

Working with Edward Larrabee Barnes was quite different. I stretched to fill his unique requirements of avoiding opulence, sensuality, and – certainly – extravagance. His was a Puritan aesthetic: Ivy League, honed down, direct, yet without the minimalist flair of the International Style. Our first assignment, designing fabrics for his Pan American 707 fleet, was such a happy experience that I asked him to design our Fifth Avenue showroom and then the campus for Haystack Mountain School of Crafts on Deer Isle, Maine, for which I was building chairman. In working with him on these projects and the Disciples of Christ seminary campus in Indiana, I observed his youthful charm bringing out the best in others. At Haystack I watched with delight as he convinced our founder and director to stretch the budget sufficiently to go quite beyond what they felt our needs to be. The result was architecture as an art form and a solution that will serve the school into the third millennium.

For the seminary, he convinced the brotherhood to postpone the central and costly chapel from the first phase to be able to afford quality in other buildings. "Someone will eventually fund a fine chapel," he reassured them. He also persuaded them to add monies from the Art Fund budget for the auditorium curtain we were to weave. "Build the art into the architecture, rather than a separate jewel laid upon it," he argued. On the other hand, when he and Mary Barnes worked on the executive interiors for his IBM Tower in New York, a project with a high budget, the restraint of our modestly priced Silky Way fabric seemed to them adequately posh. Still, when Ed asked me which trees to use for IBM's south-facing atrium and I suggested timber bamboo, he selected huge clumps of the best cultivar, which have served well, and in good scale, from opening day.

On the main floor of what was then the world's tallest building, the Sears bank in Chicago boasted enormous rooms, with fine marble on the floors and walls high enough for large trees. The sound was brutal until we installed twenty-eight quilted silk hangings with imagery reflecting the building's International Style. During installation the associate architect at Skidmore, Owings & Merrill suggested we take eight inches off the bottom of each panel. My installer's comment, "Now I know who cut the Rembrandt," ended that discussion.

Roland Terry's 1960s house for Paul Smith in Seattle illustrates the Northwest Style I learned so well during my undergraduate years there. The importance of texture, integration with outdoor living spaces, and understated elegance are key. To offset overcast skies, Terry typically sparked a neutral palette with my sunny colors. Here the upholstery is our printed stripe Cinnabar.

I first saw Frank Lloyd Wright while I was at Cranbrook, in 1950. Although he was already in his seventies, this was his first Detroit appearance, occasioned by Eliel Saarinen's death earlier that year. The humongous downtown auditorium held five thousand; eight thousand tried to attend. As Wright crossed that large stage, he filled the whole of it, while his magnetism extended over the audience. After assuring us he had built many houses in Michigan, he spoke of automotive design. "Cars should be shaped like fish and be as flexibly articulated to move in and out of traffic." He lambasted city planning, forte of the elder Saarinen: "Cities cannot be planned, but grow like tumors so one can only operate on them." He couldn't understand man's urge to congregate; there is an acre in Texas for every American, but still we huddle in cities to choke on our filth. He had heard that the world's population could stand on Bermuda but was surprised we hadn't tried it.

I saw Mr. Wright again over a year later, after my American Random Collection opened at Thaibok Ltd. I was pleased when he ordered a large yardage of my iridescent blue linen design for the meeting room at Taliesin in Wisconsin. Around the time that Larsen Incorporated opened its New York showroom on 58th Street and Park Avenue in 1954, Wright was living at the Plaza Hotel down the street. One day he called to josh me that he would not be needing my services anymore because Schumacher was producing a fabric collection based on his architectural ornament. He was going commercial with these fabrics, plus a popularly priced furniture collection bearing his signature. Licensing the use of a designer's name was not yet practiced.

The architecture and design community was incensed that a hero was so publicly cashing in the chips. Both curious and outraged, they accepted as a body for a black-tie benefit dinner honoring him at the Waldorf's Starlight Roof. On this occasion he appeared to be good-natured. He complimented interior designers on the handiwork of that evening's venue, which could never have been wonderful and was now long over the hill as well. He claimed to have just heard that among the crowd that night was the person more responsible than any other for American taste. "Would Miss Dorothy Draper please stand?" Poor Dorothy, not knowing he was pulling her leg, rose her great height and bowed to the four quarters. He then asked, "Have any of you ever tried swimming *up*stream?" He claimed he had, all his long life, until recently. Now it seemed he had come down so far, so fast, that he would that night be able to

Originally planned as a boutique collection spanning many media, Larsen World ended as a coordinated fabric collection at a modest price point. Katcha Wakisaka in our studio drew these free-flowing patterns, including my shirt and Roma, the scarf I am holding.

address us – eye to eye! This was the same level of derision he would give when the *New York Times* asked for his comment on the first European tour by four hundred of America's interior designers. "If that ship never reaches Lisbon, American design will be ahead by fifty years!"

In Miami the next week, when his furniture previewed in a showroom on Northeast 40th Street, he confided to me his chagrin at having spoken so roughly to an audience that just might have enhanced his royalties on his popular new lines. His talk there was conciliatory, but not nearly so memorable. We met just once more, when I was asked to create the window fabrics for the last house he designed, on a small island in Long Island Sound. As its dominant material was stone flecked with mica, Wright wanted a drapery related in tone and surface. I selected honey-colored tussah silk yarns, both rich and matte, then randomly brocaded over them a second layer of five different

During Edgar Kaufmann, Jr.'s lifetime, I was happy to help him find ethnographic textiles to enrich the rooms at Frank Lloyd Wright's masterpiece, Fallingwater, which had been commissioned by his parents. We filled orders for all the house's fabrics – mostly from our Doria range of handspun, handwoven wools.

While designing hangings for three walls of his Unitarian Church in Rochester, we taught architect Louis Kahn how to weave. The objective was to provide visual incident and acoustical correction for a windowless concrete cube with reflected light from above. Kahn's challenge to us was to span the full color spectrum with only one yellow, one red, and one blue yarn. By warming the yellow, then lightening the blue, I was able to achieve orange, green, and purple with the admixtures. Shown in detail, the vertical yarns are wool handspun in Mexico. The invisible horizontals are stiff, transparent monofilament to provide body. Thick batting behind the panels drinks up the sound.

French metallic gimps. Together, the silks and metals formed a heavy, timeless cloth – both opulent and understated. Briefly, until our mill closed soon after, we offered it as Celestial.

In addition to being a great architect and form giver, Louis Kahn was a charismatic, influential teacher and a lecturer determined not just to please his audience, but also to stretch them with unfamiliar concepts. I had met him with Emmanuel Benson, dean of Philadelphia Museum College (later Philadelphia College of Art), then heard his provocative lectures at design conferences and toured his Yale University Art Gallery. Our luncheon meeting at my Gramercy Park apartment in 1962 revealed more humility than I would have guessed, and a deep concern with interior detail. For his Unitarian Church at Rochester, he had created a cubic concrete space with glorious light deflected from above, but with no windows or interior detailing, and reverberating sound. He asked if we would consider making a series of hangings to correct the sound and to provide visual incident on three of the walls. This agreed, could we consider creating a color harmony with only red, blue, and yellow? I said yes, if he would allow us to use a sky blue and a very dark yellow so the three colors would have about the same value to fuse with each other. When I demonstrated this with hanks of yarn at the studio, he agreed, and was fascinated by the looms in operation. "Will you teach me to weave?" We said yes, and he was off.

For the act curtain of the Wolf Trap Theater outside Washington, D.C., we sent a nylon warp yarn to Coral Stephens in Swaziland. She densely handwove the mohair wefts to achieve a rich cloth resistant to soil and weather. At the opening, the Swazi king in full regalia sat with us in the presidential box; our fabric was his country's largest export!

My Tapestries Collection of fine china for Dansk combined classic elements of China and Europe. The embossed pattern was drawn from bamboo husks collected at Round House.

My solution was to use finger-thick handspun wool that could be made at Riggs Sargent, a studio in Mexico. It would be sound absorbing and resistant to soil and light. With it, we could shade the warp from red to gold to blend oranges, from gold to sky blue to create greens, and from blue to red to achieve light purples and mauves. We repeatedly dyed yarns until we felt we had the right shades to wrap boards for determining the color progression. We then warped a section and tried a number of wefts to find that only a clear monofilament, heavy as pencil lead and stiff as wire, would not affect the clarity of the warp colors. It produced a rigidity desirable in the vertical panels, which needed to hang out considerably from the wall in order to form a shadow line and to permit a thick, sound-absorbent batting behind them. Our presentation sent off, Louis called to say that it looked plausible, and that he would soon be over to discuss it further and take another weave lesson. However, he was currently traveling considerably. We rendered the entire progression for the three walls and waited for Kahn while letters came from the church asking if we could please be ready by Christmas, then by Easter. In Mexico, Wendell Riggs died in surgery, making it necessary to handweave the panels in New York at a cost far beyond budget. Louis finally found a date to come over and sit at the loom, so he could comprehend the process and give us approval, and we went forward. The yarn had to be spun and dyed, and as each of dozens of panels required separate warping, the process dragged on for many months. As with too many of our commissions, we absorbed the difference between cost and price.

Fortunately, we have had dozens of clients presenting new challenges to pull us past our own conventions. None have ever been more influential than Edward Wormley and Bertha Schaefer, whom I have come to consider as mentors (see pages 146–148).

BROADER FIELDS

Early on, the product design services of Larsen Design Studio were engaged by a small textile firm under the daring new leadership of Peter Kaufman. Here was the appealing challenge of an organization obviously needing a new image, market positioning, and public relations, as well as product design. Rushing into the attractive challenge of reshaping from the ground up, we succeeded in giving them a new product, while garnering some awards and good press in design publications. But we had designed a saddle pony where a sturdy workhorse was called for: with our designs, the company's sales team would have to be replaced or retrained and new buyers found. The transition could have been successfully made, but over a period of years, with patience and a great deal of mothering. As consultants we could walk away from a near disaster – only a little wiser for the experience. Interestingly enough, Peter Kaufman also learned: he went on to international success in mid-priced furnishing fabrics.

We had not fully learned that "any chain is only as strong as its weakest link." In our own firm, our small size and scant resources prevented us from making major mistakes. Here we were designers, with a boost from the then-influential design press, in an era when design – particularly new design, our design – was extremely desirable. Without being aware of it, we were moving on the crest of a great wave not of our making. In a design-driven world, others, too, thought we had the answers.

In the late fifties and before design copyrights, an early spring issue of the *New Yorker* carried similar ads from the three leading swimwear manufacturers. All featured nearly identical copies of our popular print Midsummer. Two of these giants asked if we would make patterns exclusive to them. We briefly designed prints for one of them, which were probably not as successful as that first copy by a street-smart stylist.

Next, the large downtown fabric converter Bloomcraft first printed one of our dramatic weaves, then retained our design services for several print collections. Although modern style was new to the veteran president, he had more sense of our direction than his production and sales chiefs, who always seemed to be trying to sabotage our efforts. This became a familiar pattern: Larsen Design Studio would be engaged by the top brass, then thrown to the wolves of sales heads and engineers at plants far removed from design currents. Almost without exception the engineers were convinced that their New York bosses had made a big mistake in contracting our (rival) design services. At first, when they gave repeated reasons why our innovations could not or should not go forward, we did not realize that we needed to win over these stubborn men, while repeatedly assuring the sales team that they had an invincible design package and providing them with some leads as to where it could be marketed.

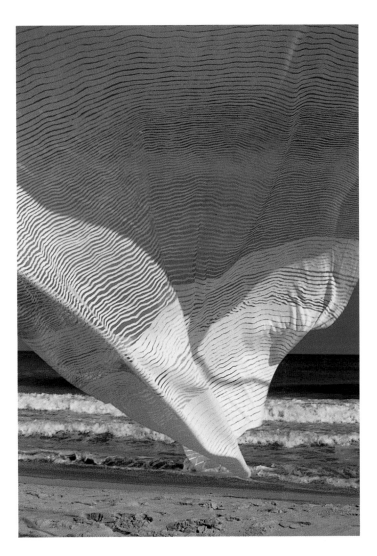

The Seascape pattern grew out of my feeling that what urban professionals needed at the end of the workday was a walk on a deserted beach. The ten-by-ten-foot pattern repeat is printed with acid on a heavy cotton cloth woven over a polyester scrim. With heat, the printed cotton burns out to expose the translucent scrim.

My retrospective exhibition in 1981, at the Musée des Arts Décoratifs at the Palais du Louvre in Paris, was divided into six square pavilions, each showing one aspect of my work. Here, the color gallery displayed nearly one hundred printed and woven cloths dominated by the color red. The bordered wool Wilton rug is Fantasy, in macédoine coloring.

Despite these challenges, some giant breakthroughs and windfalls came our way. My friend Philip Cutler, the ranking modernist at Macy's, convinced his boss to commission Bloomcraft for a major Larsen Collection, sight unseen. An order was placed for 100,000 yards of color-coordinated prints – exactly as we felt they should be. With this order in hand, Bloomcraft's sales department retreated while the production team raced to help us achieve the finished product. The result was joyous! A flower garden of vibrating modern color – not hesitant or accommodating, but a fresh breakthrough in a period when fabric departments were still of major importance in department stores.

The first surprise came on the day of the Macy's unveiling, when two hundred staff members from two sales floors were gathered to witness the bombast. Only then was it explained to these people that they were not expected to really *sell* our designs: "The new Larsen fabrics make for great windows and display rooms, advertisements, and news stories. This would bring in many new buyers – for the 'safe and sane' fabrics, which are also available."

In spite of this slur, our collection was Macy's best-selling introduction in twenty years. At Macy's in San Francisco it was still more successful. Even our architect and designer clients seemed pleased to have such fabrics available where they could confidently direct friends and family. Bolstered with all this good news, I called Bloomcraft's Midwest sales manager with key accounts such as Marshall Field and J. L. Hudson. To my "How are we doing?" he responded, "Oh, I didn't show your collection to them, didn't feel they would like it." Therefore, a considerable success was not the landslide it might have been: both we and Bloomcraft had counted too much on design alone, not on the total effort required.

Our reputation for design innovations and full-blown color brought many to the showroom. Clients such as Marilyn Monroe quickened the heartbeat of our male staff. Others came shopping not to buy, but for inspiration to fuel New York's Seventh Avenue. With the advent of copyright protection, we learned how to police our line from knockoffs, usually after the fact. When a store would innocently advertise dresses in our patterns, we would order an injunction against the store, the fashion house, and, if we knew it, the printer as well. Not wanting to be branded a coy house, the store would join our suit, and success was ensured. This meant the pattern would have to be off the market in twenty-four hours. We also released news of this victory to the press. Word was out that "although the management cannot expect stylists to stop copying, they shouldn't copy Larsen; it gets our name in the papers."

Although collecting damages through the lawsuits that followed took longer, we were sufficiently successful to cover our legal fees. One amusing case involved a young firm called Glenn of Michigan. They reproduced our patterns rather faithfully until we enjoined them not to. Later, to make sure they were behaving, we sent my assistant, posing as a buyer, to their showroom. They were selling from our samples of new designs – including architect Warren Platner's spectacular stripe, Cinnabar. When our lawyer, Lee Epstein, called their attorney, also a Mr. Epstein, his answer was, "We know that Jack Larsen invented flowers – but stripes?"

At my exhibition at the Louvre, one gallery was given over to commissions and special projects, such as my colorful upholsteries for Braniff Airlines, shown here on mocked-up seats. With the objective of maximizing variations within each cabin, the soft worsted damask stripes modulate down the back and across the seat. Almost imperceptibly, the color also progresses from the front to the back of the cabin.

Painted Plains, printed on tussah silk for our Terra Nova Collection, is shown here in the den of Linda and Stanley Marcus's adobe home in Santa Fe.

We also sold fabric to leading fashion designers including Pauline Trigère, B. H. Wragge, and Donald Brooks. Sometimes this was successful, but most designers then were managed by a "bad brother" in the back room, determined to end the season with no fabric inventory. What was not sold came back months later as "flawed." An exception was Jax of California, a fresh young company selling design the way we did, and remote from Seventh Avenue business practice. With Jax we gained colorful pages in *Life* magazine and the attention of the influential Kennedy family.

When the heady colors, new patterns, and lush ground cloths of our printed fabrics found wide appeal, friends and board members felt called on to speed our growth through diversification. "Your cloths would be so wonderful to wear! Why not design apparel?" And why not? I felt we could do better than the tube skirts of our printed velvet cloths so many architects' wives wore for evening. Certainly, this was the kind of challenge I most enjoyed. Perhaps I could design the classic clothes women "above fashion" dreamed of: comfortable, becoming, timeless. Only the cloths would change from season to season.

And I did, naming the line J. L. Arbiter. Close-fitting through the bodice and with long, thin sleeves, our A-line coat-dresses made a size fourteen look and feel like a ten – without a waist cinch. They looked right for daywear or theater, in town and out, without seasonal limitation. The unconstructed jackets of handspun cloths had this same universality. Although the coats sold less well, their architectural cuts and unique cloths also set them apart. My reversible tube of channel-quilted silk taffeta was the first down-filled coat on the market.

The small boutique in one arm of our Fifth Avenue show-room attracted press and then celebrity clients. A disappointment came from the *Vogue* editors who had been so encouraging. They returned to comment that the classic wardrobe had been such a great idea, what was I going to do next? When Neiman Marcus and I. Magnin each market-tested a hundred sample garments and then came back with a large order, we had to make the decision to quickly grow much larger, or stop. We stopped. I had learned that a designer does not enter the apparel market with only one hand. It had been great fun dreaming of evening wear one night, beach gear the next, but such a broad focus hardly made for a viable business. I was consoled by our senior staff asking that I not stop having "crazy ideas," and by Joan Baez asking if I would go on making things just for her. That I could not do.

Instead we embarked on a new adventure. Ja-el Fabrics focused on Seventh Avenue designers, including Donald Brooks and Gerald Pierce. A telling moment came when Chester Weinberg's magnificent opera coats in our velvet batiks caused a standing ovation at the end of his runway show. Buyers and editors, who had chatted through the showing as if nothing was going on, actually gasped. Soon the coats were in Bergdorf Goodman's Fifth Avenue windows. Next, they were closed out at Loehmann's.

Believing that we now understood design for the retail market of department stores and furniture manufacturers, we launched a junior line for this larger market. My dream had become to design simple but honest, delightfully colored fabrics

Étoile, my hand-woven silk upholstery for Baker Furniture, imparts opulence to this multicushioned sofa. The cloth was color-woven in ombré stripes, then discharge-printed to replace the stripe color with the almost metallic gold of the Baroque motif.

Illustrated above are the very first linens produced by our silk weavers in Thailand. The silvery wet-spun line-linen yarns permit these sun-resistant sheers, enriched by hand-craft techniques. Swan Song (top) is a shower of pearly silk strands falling over a scrim. In City Blocks (right) heavy silk is brocaded over sheer linen, then cleanly clipped. Lindos is an architectural fenestration pattern translated into three densities of linen gauze.

Right: The most recent of our silk and linen cloths handcrafted in Thailand is Onward!, which defies the definition of weaving as a horizontal/vertical structure. The six-inch-wide bands of creamy silk are woven obliquely over a warp of wetspun linen.

at a "dollar a yard," targeted at a lower income bracket. We focused our sights on those stores and furniture makers appealing to youthful, upscale consumers. The press was favorable, for here was design available to all readers. So were retailers. We launched the line with five major windows at both Bloomingdale's in New York and Carson's in Chicago.

When Richard Himmel, the fashionable Chicago decorator, ordered seven thousand yards of the fabric that he had seen in Carson's windows for a hotel, it seemed for a moment as if we had achieved *both* markets. But then trouble began. To keep this new division distinct from the pricier collection, we had named it for our associate, Win Anderson. Without warning us, Bloomingdale's signed displays with my name instead. Within weeks they wanted to see a new collection markedly different from the first. In two months, when we still felt the first group was newborn, store markdowns began – causing their retail price to fall below our wholesale. If we had been older and larger, we may have been able to obtain agreements controlling some of these discounts, or have been seasoned enough to anticipate the ongoing power struggle between manufacturers and retailers, or have hired someone with the savvy and tough attributes required. This is what design licensing has since achieved. Although the license is too often little more than exploitation of a name, some fine collaborations have come about. At least designers and manufacturer-distributors focus on what they do best.

More to the point, perhaps, has been the parallel development of in-store designer boutiques. I well remember the frustrations of designers such as B. H. Wragge, who every season had created wardrobes in which each garment seamlessly complemented the others. In the store, the blouse made for a suit would be in another department, the matching coat on another floor. Showing all of the pieces together is such an obvious plus for all concerned that one wonders why it was so long in coming.

Our design licensing came early and has continued with mixed success. The earliest to be successful was our Fine Arts Towel Collection for J. P. Stevens in 1966, the first designer collection in the bed-and-bath arena. We were greatly aided by friend Everett Brown's revolutionary color program at Fieldcrest. As a consultant, Brown had reached out to sales clerks by sending jars of chutney to their homes with a letter explaining mangoes and the exotic spices that Columbus had sought. "Soon they would have chutney-colored towels to offer, and shocking pink ones the color of Siamese silk." This ploy worked. On a grassroots level, Brown opened American eyes to the pleasures of weaver Dorothy Liebes's "Chinatown Colors."

Knowing this, I could continue his leadership. When Stevens was just entering the towel arena to complement the company's Utica sheets, I convinced them to consider Fieldcrest's sales of full-bodied color, *not* the pale primroses generally sold. My analysis was that in towels – unlike rugs and sofas – no color shade was too high style because "mistakes" could be hidden in linen closets.

When patterned towels were printed, we chose jacquard weaves so boldly colored that no buyers could overlook them. As weavers, we found terry cloth quite miraculous in transforming a thin, dull yarn into a resilient, lush velvet. We also discovered that the surface could be solid on one side and striped on the other. In jacquard patterns the solid and shaded stripes could be combined. On the loom, with all the yarns starched like fine wires, these towels look like mosquito netting. With washing the loops open like tight buds becoming blossoms. At Colonial Williamsburg, where we introduced the collection to the sales team, models paraded in wearing loungewear and beach togs Gerald Pierce had designed with the towels. The response was enthusiastic, as it was in the stores. In months, these became America's best-selling bath towels.

Often called "the natural fiber man," I also enjoy working with new technology and man-made yarns for a fresh aesthetic. The silver fabric shown here is our solar cloth, a warp-knit polyester that is heat-set, then coated with aluminum powder to reduce heat transfer by 60 percent. Nimbus, on the right, is a casement cloth woven of Saran monofilament, then shrunk to achieve its wafflelike dimension.

LEARNING HOW TO SEE

As drawing had never been my forte in school and watercolor renderings were particularly trying, I attempted to illustrate architectural schemes and furniture designs with models. With model making I had some skill and a keener sense of the dimensional space visible from several vantage points. Later, when I had finally mastered weaving, I adopted a hypothesis that we have a natural aptitude for drawing, in two dimensions, or building, in three. As I was comfortably confident in the latter, my scant drawing skills deteriorated the more I worked on fabric patterns through a draftsman, including such great ones as Don Wight and Paul Gedeohn.

As an undergraduate I had a superb teacher in a tall, athletic Englishwoman named Charlotte Curtis. In short order she analyzed my drawing as being "in the fingers." Out came black ink, an oversize pointed brush with a long handle, and her command to "observe closely, hold the charged brush firmly by the handle tip to record in bold strokes the essence of a geranium plant." It worked! I could easily capture the nature of the leaf, the thrust of its stem, the joining of stem and trunk, and of trunks to ground. Amazingly, the drawings took on a style related to the ground-ink drawings of East Asia. Even then, newsprint was so affordable that I could quickly attempt one approach after another, making the strokes by moving my whole arm from the shoulder.

As I developed some skill with the brush, my eye quickened as well. Why was this joining right, and that one false? This plant growing and that one, at best, broken at soil level? Once learned, this ability to analyze, to feel visual relationships, was not forgotten. I sensed balance if it existed and a means of achieving it where it did not, in three dimensions as well as in two.

In this process no tool or method has been more useful than comparison. First, I learned to get work off the loom or drawing board, into another light and at some distance from its creation. I would try to enumerate all of the options, then to weave the most likely ones, pinning them up to compare the results at some distance, perhaps in different lights, on horizontal and vertical surfaces. I asked, "Why is one superior to the others? What do they all lack?" In working with assistants, students, and clients I found most people can select the best

of a group and can explain their preference, if asked. "I like" is, of course, the key phrase; it indicates a response. The next important step is, "I prefer this one *because,*" or "I don't respond to any *because.*" First feeling; then analysis.

But what is the quality of the response? Is it only associative, reminding one of an earlier experience? Or is the response to the presentation rather than the content? We are told, "Don't judge a book by its cover!" But in the visual arena, we usually do. Look again! What is the concept, what is the statement? Or is it the coloring? Most of us, at all levels of sophistication, respond first and foremost to color. Color is the first and final determinant in almost every purchasing decision.

As a student I learned the most from Hope Foote, my tough and relentless interior architecture professor. I credit her with being the only one who taught taste – but how? Not, I believe, in her drawing boldly over my renderings still damp from an all-night charrette. She was unknowingly best at our weekly critiques. Getting our work off the drawing board and onto a wall helped; so did seeing it in comparison to other attempts to resolve the same assignment. Miss Foote seldom analyzed. Almost tongue-tied, she gestured and pointed, mumbled, frowned, or nodded approval. I, at least, would think out her script. What was resolved? What had nuance? Where was there a concept or a consistent integrity, a harmony, deeper than stylish presentation? In short, where was taste?

What defines taste or lack of it? Taste is elusive, a simple thing, neither puffed up nor pretentious. Taste is positive and not just the absence of the bad-mannered. Taste allows a fillip or flair, even broken rules or a visual pun. Taste is not high-flown, does not call attention to itself, and has nothing to do with Sunday clothes, company manners, or cost. Indeed, extravagant elements are apt to call attention to themselves. As expressions, both "good taste" and "bad taste" seem irrelevant: there is taste and, alas, the lack of it.

What a boon when Mark Tobey invited me to his studio! At the door he greeted me by saying, "I've never met a weaver before, but have known some potters" (Bernard Leach and Chimei Hamada, with whom he had spent a year in Japan). We did not discuss Tobey's work but rather his small collection of favorite objects. "Close your eyes until I get this piece against a gray wall," he would say. Then he explained how neutral, middle-value gray would reduce the importance of the silhouette so that I would be more aware of the content, the relationship of parts to the whole, the essence. "No! Don't blow the dust off!"

When he asked me to bring over some of my work, I marveled at how he read meaning into tensions below the cloth surface. From architecture I had learned to understand a cloth in relation to furniture, to a room and its occupants. Where I had contrasted smooth yarns against those that were soft and light-absorbing, Tobey read these contrasts as the harmony of yin and yang, or of rocks and water in the landscape. Over coffee sipped from tea bowls we discussed the meaning of art as being an expression of all of life.

Without a doubt the breakthrough in my learning how to see occurred in Tokyo in the early 1980s. I was met on arrival by Ichiro Saito and a young friend of his, who came as escorts to the Hukudaya Ryokan, the inn recommended by Isamu Noguchi. As we dined in my rooms, Saito announced that he and I would perform the tea ceremony the next morning with a famous tea master. When I protested that this was the only aspect of Japanese culture that left me cold, Saito replied that we would be leaving quite early to visit the most famous master of the reformed tea ceremony, who was also a collector and an accomplished potter. Further, he promised that we would be joined by Toshiko Horiuchi, a beautiful weaver we both knew well.

After sunrise on a clear winter day, Toshiko, Saito, and I traveled by underground and then by train to a pleasant residential suburb and the small traditional house of master Shoan Komori. Neither casual nor formal, our welcome was that of the awaited. At eighty, our host spoke quietly and assuredly in English. His flawless presence and youthful body movements were disarming. As pared down as his shaven head, his slender body and clear eyes, his grayed-out kimono (understated in its *shibui* taste), and his every gesture suggested that we were not where we belonged.

We were introduced to his solemn daughter, then invited to sit on the tatami floor of the largest room, pleasantly day-lit through shoji screens. His daughter, in the absence of a son, was his successor as tea master. Of the small boxes containing ritual tea objects that she opened, the first and "most lowly" were his own ceramics, mainly tea bowls made at the famous potteries of Bizen, Seto, and Shigaraki. He explained the reason for a heavily weighted foot or a soft transition as being the result of his response to working a creamy clay body, and the meaning of a stroke of slip or a soft blush on the glaze as a "gift of the fire." As he shared this intimate history and his daughter quietly and

reverently opened box after box, time was forgotten. There was space for responses, then the pleasure he expressed in our comprehension.

I noticed that as we moved on to viewing works not of his making, their storage boxes encased in silk were of finer workmanship. These housed water jars and flower containers, some Chinese and many of venerable age. He explained that the point was not the objects or their history and worth, but our perception of them. He would ask, "Can we perceive these clay particles washed for thousands of years by the waters of a receding lake? Can we observe the kindly impression of this Sung potter's left thumb? Do these few brushstrokes of white slip convey to us the potter's joy in the perfume of quince blossoms after a cold northern winter?"

Perception, I was learning, required focusing an inner eye so untrammeled by the world outside as to be intensely infused with the present. This seems so simple and natural but, without preparation, it is unobtainable, even when we search for meaning at museums or temples. Perceiving lies in comprehending the whole, the essence of an object, not just its outline or another superficial aspect. Attaining perception resembles the hoped-for understanding in the ritual of taking communion. The value is not in becoming one with an object (or, as in the writings of Walt Whitman, with a blade of grass), but in being one with a universe both more vast and more intimate than is known by science.

Finally, the daughter quietly set out five similar black lacquered boxes, almost square, but with the faces of each box a quadrangle imperceptibly different from the others. As we observed them in silence, the master addressed me. "Although all of these are ancient and by the same maker, one is more perfect in its beauty and therefore more precious than all the others. Can you perceive which one it is?" As my eyes observed the five forms, I remembered something Edgar Kaufmann once told me: "Although we now know that Titian overpainted *A Man with a White Glove* a dozen times, on the same canvas, Picasso often painted the same subject a dozen times on different canvases. Perhaps only in the next century will we know which is the real one. Then all the others will fall away as precursors."

And then I knew! It was as if one box towered over the others, radiating with an inner light. For this short interval of time I understood perception as a cosmic experience. Although the master's approval was not needed, I gratefully received it as we stood up, accepted an outer garment, and made ready to enter his miniature garden.

A tea garden, I learned, provides a prescribed path for approaching the teahouse. A water basin is there for purification, a bench for awaiting a quiet state of mind; perhaps an awareness of the fortuitous opening of a camellia blossom or some other seasonal "gift" prepares us to enter. The minuscule teahouse, in the style of sixteenth-century tea master Sen no Rikyu, embodied perfection. As we came into its two-tatami room the tea master and his daughter, who would officiate, bowed a welcome. The father sat opposite her, and the three of us in front of them. First, he explained the ritual objects chosen for that day. The hanging scroll in the tokonoma alcove was a rare example by a seventeenth-century Chinese poet. Only through good fortune had he found the flower container below it, glaze-painted by the same artist. Still sparkling with dew, the flowers in it were identical blossoms to those in the painting. And so on: each of the room's appointments carried an underlying, interconnected message.

Hot water was dipped from the iron pot to a ewer, then poured to warm and cleanse the tea bowl, and then poured out. The bowl was refilled and powdered tea added to be whisked to a frothy green brew. Following his lead, we each examined the bowl while turning it in our hands to contemplate its fragrant content. We tilted the bowl with both hands, drank, passed on the bowl, and meditated, only dimly aware that the implements were being cleaned and restored to place.

He broke the silence by asking, "Is there anything else you would like?" He spoke so convincingly that I felt comfortable in asking if we could do it again. So we did, in silence and with still deeper meaning, to the effect of its being the most religious experience I have ever known. Here was the marriage of beauty and faith I had so long awaited! That it was also on the deepest level of bonding with friends enhanced a great sense of wholeness.

Outside and back into time, the master invited us for a soba lunch before we boarded the train. As we finished our buckwheat noodles and focused on Asian pears, I asked him how I could return his favor. He answered, "If you can, please send Mozart's *Magic Flute* conducted by Karl Böhm." As we moved toward the train platform and performed farewell bows, I asked where I could find handcrafted straw sandals as beautiful as his but in my size. The tea master's wisdom extended even to the smallest concerns: "Go where the sumo wrestlers shop; they have large feet and can afford the best."

DESIGNING IN THE NINETIES

While my artist friends seem to cherish most the work they have just completed, I enjoy most what I am only conceptualizing. I also open incoming strike-offs with the enthusiasm of a child at Christmas. On the other hand, as activities from previous seasons take on the lackluster of the recent past, they are little mentioned here.

This does not mean the last ten years have seen a slowing down in any way. Rather, improved communications have turned the 1990s into a frenzied period. I had enjoyed the telex keeping us in touch with team players across the world, avoiding telephone tag and leaving a brief record of what had been said. I do not like responding to faxes only to be obliged to answer the incoming reply an hour later.

One of the brighter lights of the nineties has been increased work in Asia. While Japan today is a splendid place to develop textiles at the cutting edge, it is occasionally a major market as well. What a treat to walk into the Park Hyatt Hotel high on top of Kenzō Tange's three towers joined by sky bridges! Designer John Morford has made this world-class hotel a Larsen museum with our fabric and furniture in almost every area. Each year, too, I marvel at new wonders in booming Southeast Asia, and I enjoy participating in the dawn of modern jacquard silk weaving in India. Among our many commissions, I relished designing carpets for Meany Hall at my alma mater and, more recently, fabric and carpets for Benaroya Hall, new home of the Seattle Symphony.

At my company we felt we must replace a longtime president, then impeach his successor. Frank Huggins came out of retirement to help us identify Phil Cooper as the leader who created a turnaround and worked out a merger with the English firm Colefax and Fowler – all in time for my big seventieth-birthday celebration at LongHouse.

Now a design consultant to my own firm and others, I am occasionally free to ask, "What would I most like to do today?" The answer remains, "I most enjoy what I don't know how to do yet."

For the 1996 renovation of Meany Hall at the University of Washington I devised a large-scale carpet pattern in clear colors to be in step with the cavernous spaces and brutal materials. The glass sculpture in related color shades is by my friend Dale Chihuly.

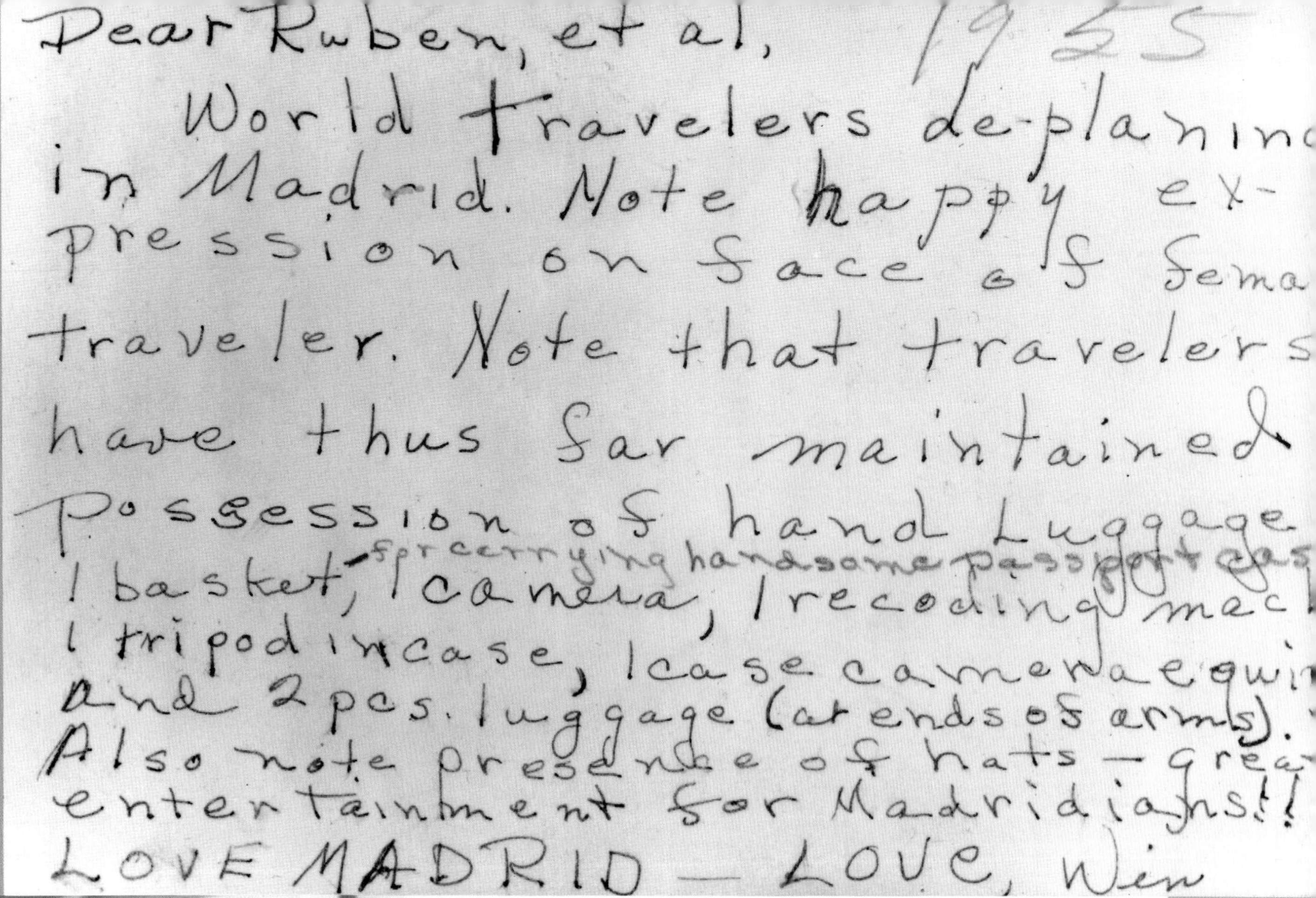

Dear Ruben, et al,   1955

World travelers de-planing
in Madrid. Note happy ex-
pression on face of fema[le]
traveler. Note that travelers
have thus far maintained
possession of hand luggage
1 basket - for carrying handsome passport cas[e]
1 camera, 1 recoding mac[hine]
1 tripod in case, 1 case camera equi[p]
and 2 pcs. luggage (at ends of arms).
Also note presence of hats — grea[t]
entertainment for Madridians!!
LOVE MADRID — LOVE, Win

Jack Larsen and Win Anderson arriving in Madrid, 1955.

EUROPE   By my mid-twenties I had lectured or exhibited in most North

American cities and worked in Haiti, Mexico, and Peru. Although I felt disad-

vantaged in not knowing Europe at all, I did not want to go until I could make

it an open-ended trip. In April of 1954 my friend Bill Pahlman organized the

first Interior Design Tour of Europe, with many opportunities too good to

miss. ■ The morning sailing party was phenomenal. The maiden voyage of the

Olympia was the first sailing of a Greek liner from the New World to Athens.

Greek royalty were aboard; so were the grandes dames of interior design.

Against the backdrop of steamer trunks being lifted aboard by cranes and the

delivery of orchids and champagne hampers, it was as festive as a great ball, and

only the beginning. A few of my friends were there as well. One of our staff members wept openly – not because I was leaving, but because she was not. Phyllis Hoffzimer, a young client I toasted with as we passed the Statue of Liberty, marveled that multitudes had greeted her prayerfully, while we were delighted to wave farewell!

In the Bay of Naples we were awakened early and transferred to motor launches to take us to Capri. Sunny, full of flowers and smiling faces, freely bohemian in spirit, Capri was a perfect antidote to the confinement aboard ship. Phyllis and I practiced our newly learned Italian with the café staff and visited the museum/house of the famous Swedish doctor Axel Munte. I enjoyed it all so much that I stayed on alone. That night I visited Bricktop's lively club, watched the moon rise over the Mediterranean, and then found a *pensione*. Taking a steamer to the mainland the next morning, I hitched a hair-raising ride around the serpentine Amalfi drive with some local youths on motor scooters.

In Rome we enthusiastically toured classical ruins, Renaissance palaces and the Vatican, the fountains at Trevi, and modern luxury on Via Condotti, where I ordered suits and a coat at Cucci, ties from Son and Man Arbiter, and custom shoes from Valentino. The balcony of my hotel room overlooked the Spanish Steps. I made friends with the young manager there, who helped me to buy a secondhand Vespa and to learn to ride it. This popular little vehicle gave me the freedom and independence I so much craved.

The Eternal City was buzzing with Vespas driven by young men with their girls decorously riding sidesaddle behind them, or even parents with two children and a dog balanced on the running board. But it was the corpulent old cardinals in blazing red habits that convinced me that I too could manage one, even through Italian traffic. I moved with no rules except not to hit anyone.

From Rome onward, the English-language newspaper carried stories of our design pilgrimage. We would soon be off to Siena and Florence, it said, and we were. While the tour's deluxe coaches rolled through Pisa, I headed to Orvieto for a trattoria lunch washed down with the famous stone-dry *vino*. I ascended several of the other walled hill towns seeking a hotel or *pensione,* and finally I asked a postmaster for one. "There are none," he said, "but you can stay with me and my schoolteacher daughter. You'd like her; she speaks English and has the only

motor vehicle in the area, a Lambretta." That evening the daughter and I held hands through the daredevil high-wire acts of a one-ring circus, in which the same seven people collected tickets, provided music, performed animal acts, rode bareback, and accomplished phenomenal feats on a high trapeze without nets. For a small sum, we had tickets for the mayor's box.

On the road to Siena the next day I observed few cars, scooters, or even carriages, but only lumbering oxcarts. Most of the people I saw were swineherdesses driving free-ranging hogs over the steep hillsides to develop the solid muscle fiber needed for prosciutto. The pleasant, familiar sound of simple power looms clacking away in the barns was cheery. Then, as now, I loved the lay of the land in Siena, but found Florence treeless and arid, however rich its holdings as a museum city. As I took a back route through hamlets and farmlands from Florence to my lodging in nearby Montecatini, I was impressed by the locals' practice of walking along the roads arm-and-arm or hand-in-hand, whether they were women, men, or couples. After joining our group for tours of the Baptistery, the Medici tombs, and other standard destinations, I headed off to the Uffizi Gallery alone. As it was completely empty, I spent most of the day there, turning lights on and off while passing through each of the galleries. Only when I mounted my Vespa to drive off did the guards chase after me; the museum had been closed that day!

The *autostrada* to Bologna followed a Roman road that originally was constructed to avoid the ambush of troops on the march. The only traffic was cargo trucks, which I raced with some success. They would toot while passing on the downhill run, but I could beep back while overtaking them on the way up.

Venetia was flat and an easy ride. Arriving in Venice, I found the first high-rise parking garages with steep spiral ramps, something of a challenge on two wheels. Bill Pahlman had arranged for two spectacular events there. One was a grand ball hosted by Elsie Lee, the Countess Gazzi, who owned the Fortuny print works on the island of Giudecca. Townspeople lined the street to watch our arrival by royal barges. Elsie received us in a salon draped with her new pattern, Olympia, named for the ship of our Atlantic crossing. Then she ushered us into the gardens, which were lined with tree roses. Orchestras were tuning up on three terraces lighted with a thousand Danish lanterns, and the supper tables were laid for six hundred. I felt like Cinderella at the ball as the nobility of northern Italy arrived to join in an enchanted evening. We departed in the small hours with bunches of violets to which Elsie had added a note: "From my garden." Later I learned from the Fortuny agent in Boston that the whole garden, including the blooming tree roses and young vegetables, had been installed during the three previous days.

The other special treat was a tour of the Palladian villas around Vicenza, hosted by a handsome young duke who was a friend of Pahlman's. My favorite of these remains the Villa at Stra, where Napoleon had stayed, with great ceilings painted by Tiepolo. Hosted by the mayor and local aristocracy, our luncheon banquet was in Palladio's Basilica at Vicenza, where an orchestra played Vivaldi on antique instruments. Having drunk numerous glasses of wine, I dozed in a park for so long that I missed our coach back to Venice. After taking the wrong train and not having my passport, I was summarily put off at the Austrian frontier; the mountains were cold and there was no station in sight. I finally returned on a troop train with drowsy, good-natured soldiers laid out on wooden four-tiered berths.

As our group planned to travel by train to Nice, I decided to go along because it seemed an easier way to take the Vespa into France. Getting it from the garage, into a gondola, and across the Grand Canal to the station was not simple, but we did it. In the middle of the night I was awakened by customs men repeatedly saying *"vente mille,"* and I kept saying that I didn't have that much lire. I thought they were asking for duty on my scooter, but all they were saying was, "We are at the border town of Ventimiglia, please show your passport."

The greatest pleasure in Nice was not visiting Monte Carlo or Monaco, but staying in the same hotel room that Raoul Dufy had painted so often, directly in line above a fountain in the park leading to the palm-fringed Mediterranean beyond. A designer friend rented a scooter so that we could visit the Chapelle du Rosaire, with its stained-glass windows and ceramic "drawings" by Henri Matisse, in Vence. From there we toured around mountainsides given over to fragrance farms on our way to Romanesque chapels with ancient murals.

In Arles I made the mistake of drinking all the wine that I was served, so I had too long a siesta. It was late when I raced through the papal palaces at Avignon, and I was caught in a thunderstorm before arriving in Nîmes, where our group was lodging. I took off my wet clothes and went to sleep, determined to rise early enough to borrow some money from friends. Upon rising, I saw the tour buses pass out of the gate. I struck out alone, but when my road ended in a pasture, I checked the map to find I had been following indications for a railway, not a highway! I decided to cable for some money, but found there were no cable transfers on Saturday and that Monday was a holiday. A helpful citizen took me to the mayor, who loaned me exactly enough cash for a third-class ticket to Paris, while holding my return plane ticket as collateral. On the train I awoke to find the compartment was cold and we were not moving. The car was detached and parked in a railyard! I scaled the fence into a tiny plaza where the only lighted house was a brothel. So I rescaled the fence, put on the few articles of clothing I had, and shivered until a morning train departed. Thirty hours later, half starved, I arrived in Paris.

The best parts of Paris were the nightlife of jazz on Seine houseboats, the famous chanteuse Patachou, and the Folies-Bergère. Parisians were still poor from the aftermath of the war, and Americans were unpopular with them. As the idea of crating the Vespa and arranging transport for it was forbidding, I decided to give it to the nice newsman outside my hotel. When he seemed uncertain, I gave him the bill-of-sale and license. That adventure was over, or so I thought. In New York six months later, two huge FBI men entered my studio, showed their badges, and asked me to sit down. "Did you steal a Vespa in Rome and abandon it in Paris?" It seemed the newsman, still frightened of possessing hot goods, had taken the Vespa to the Italian Embassy in Paris. From there it was traced to the dealer in Rome, who said it was stolen. Fortunately, I had heard from the hotel manager with whom I bought it and had given him a loan to help buy an inn in the mountains. The FBI cabled him, and he confirmed my innocence.

Of a hundred trips to Europe the most memorable were that first one and another long sojourn with Win in 1957. It started with my assignment to write a thirty-five-page report on the eleventh Triennale di Milano, an international design exposition, for *Interiors* magazine. Win would join me later to drive to Venice and through Yugoslavia to the Athens Festival and the Greek Isles.

Interiors was then one of the great design journals documenting the fever pitch of the Modern movement. Olga Gueft, the editor, was a fine writer and eminently successful because she understood the large picture, with its focus on creativity from both sides of the Atlantic. She believed in designers as visionaries and entrepreneurs, and I took as a command her selecting me to write such a major story. As she walked me through reportage

For the 1957, 1961, and 1964 Triennale design exhibitions in Milan I was guest editor for the pivotal magazine *Interiors*. On these occasions I spent a fortnight working with an Italian photographer with a huge old 8 x 10 camera. In between shots I tested photo angles with this small 35mm. I also made friends with some of the great design talents of Europe.

of the Triennales of 1951 and 1954, she explained what I could expect and why, which innovators to watch out for, and which Milanese architects could fill me in on the lay of the land. Her introductions included Dr. Antoluci, the photographer who had agreed to work with me for ten days.

That year's Triennale was spectacular, with pavilions by twenty nations and dramatic Italian exhibits on a number of themes. With a young Argentine interpreter, Sam Soler, running interference, I photographed the whole of it with Dr. Antoluci and two assistants. They would take an hour or more setting up each shot with a huge old box camera. Then, up on top of ladders and ready to shoot, they would decide it was time for coffee! I met Kaj Franck and Voulko Escolin from the Finnish pavilion and many Italians, including Bruno and Jacqueline Danese, who opened their famous gallery that year. The dollar was strong then, and the prices – when Soler could ferret them out – were the manufacturer's wholesale. I bought heavily, including the entire Sardinian exhibit. It was a very fine time.

When Win arrived, she took on the task of trying to finalize the Yugoslavian trip. In New York they had readily sold us the in-tourist exchange required by Eastern bloc countries, but now, when phoning Belgrade, the message was unpromising: "The road is blocked, but may be open when you get there." In Venice we attempted passage on a freighter stopping along the coast, then decided to drive down to Naples and sail from there. We watched the Italian Line ship being loaded with luxury cars for the Arab passengers, stopped for a day in Syracuse, and made friends with a couple from Beirut who were building banks and hotels there.

Athens was a dream city then, small, with few cars and no pollution. The Turkish quarter was full of bazaars and the museums were uncrowded. I thought I knew the architecture of the Acropolis from models at school. Surprise! The scale had been misleading. The Parthenon steps being a meter high, the classic buildings take on an unexpected majesty. The first Athens festival took place in the ancient Dionysian theater at the foot of the Acropolis, the perfect setting for both music and the National Greek theater. As the young Maria Callas was to make a triumphant return to Athens, the organizers hoped she would favor them with a reduced fee. Instead she charged more than Bruno Walter and the Vienna orchestra. The Greek audience glittered with diamond jewelry and tiaras, chinchilla, and ermine.

This was the second year of organized cruises from the Greek islands; we had booked two first-class cabins but were shown into crew's quarters in the ship's triangular prow. We hoped to be transferred, until at lunch we met others with cabins under the engine room and below the waterline. The food was miserable, but dancing each night with young Greek anthropologists lightened the heart. We had hoped for some relaxation, but were ashore at seven each morning for a long day's instruction. When the sun rose in Crete, a tall-masted schooner was moored next to us; it was Aristotle Onassis showing Callas the Greek Isles.

Each morning found both ships in a new harbor. Verdant Rhodes, with its million butterflies and crystalline seawater, was a perfect haven. The best-preserved building was a crusader's fort Mussolini had restored as a summer palace. On burros we ascended the acropolis, on a cliff high above the sea and the markets. At Patmos we visited the ancient monastery where the archbishops of Greek Orthodoxy had come in the 1400s after the sack of Constantinople. The great golden halls were filled with bishops in white robes and tall miters. When a tall lady in our group complained to the abbot about a stocky Greek speaking so loudly to the bishops, his response was, "If this offends you, why not move to another chamber?" The Greek was their patron, Aristotle Onassis.

SOUTH AMERICA

Of my eight trips to South America since the fifties, the most memorable was the second visit to Peru on the occasion of Chan Khan's briefly opening a small studio there to make Larsen prints for that market. As I was at that time researching for our Andean Collection, there were visits back to the Lima museums, to archaeological sites, to the Amazon, and to the highlands. Cuzco was a wonder for the Inca stonework, the brilliant flowers, and the extraordinary churches in a parade of styles, from the Moorish domes of Pizarro's time to Spanish Gothic and exuberant Baroque. Even better than the high altars paved with gold, I remember an amazing lectern many meters high, cantilevered above the stone floor. Carved in cedarwood over a lifetime by an Indian convert, it displayed imaginary heavens above the reader's head. Below, a three-dimensional filigree tapering like an inverted cone portrayed all too vividly the agonies of Purgatory. Below this lay the Tortures of Hell, but the lowest finial was the head of Martin Luther!

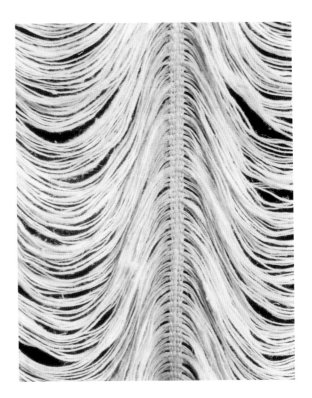

Bahia Blind from the Brazil Collection achieves a strong silhouette and a fine shadow pattern by weaving heavy slubbed linen through spaced warps with leno binding.

If Cuzco is full of reminders of terror, human bondage, and the Inquisition, Machu Picchu, four thousand feet down the Andes by way of a narrow-gauge railroad, is paradisiacal. "Is it," I wondered, "the most beautiful of cities because it is devoid of people?" No: Pompeii is also unpopulated; so are many archaeological sites in the Americas. The setting within the lower Andes is spectacular; the lush green meadows between the roofless buildings contribute, so does the eternal spring that exists at an elevation of eight thousand feet near the equator. I remember so well the euphoria caused by descending from the much higher altitude of Cuzco, of wanting to bolt up the nearby peak of Huana Picchu.

The next ascent was to be Lake Titicaca in the Bolivian Andes. When, en route, our plane put down at the Arequipa in southern Peru, the landing gear was jammed. Word came through that, instead of ruining their new landing strip, we would belly dive on the desert. And we did, without anyone being seriously hurt. Then designer Gerald Pierce and I spotted a native Peruvian with a burro walking through the desert shrubs, quite unconcerned with the plane or its passengers now huddled in the shade of its wings. After following him for some distance we came to a sleepy village where a number of men were gathered with a sense of excitement. One was holding a golden object flashing in the sunlight. Familiar with Pre-Columbian gold, we pressed closer to find this roadless hamlet now had a Lions Club insignia!

As we returned to our plane, a small aircraft was landing to see what was going on. They admitted to being en route to Lima and were able to take us with them. Gerald and I scrambled into the hold to retrieve luggage and be on our way. I don't know if the others reached Bolivia; we did not.

When we returned to Lima, Gerald went back to New York, and I to Brazil. The purpose of my visit there was twofold. The easy part was our assignment to design fabrics for Varig Airlines. My charge was stated, "to come learn about the luxury and elegance of Brazil. Without such an experience, no North American can comprehend such sophistication." I had heard over the years that the upper classes of South America felt that North Americans were polyglot plebeians. Through Dean Benson at the Philadelphia College of Art I had met Aloisio Magalenes, an artist from an old family in Recife who would go on to design Brazil's stamps and currency but at that time was deeply involved with planning the new capital at Brasília. As Brazil then produced neither furnishing textiles nor fabric designers, he asked me to design fabrics for the new buildings.

In Rio I spent a glorious week with aristocratic northern Brazilians working on this great cause. The excitement was contagious, as each day they sought news of progress at the new capital a thousand kilometers into the interior. I met the jolly, world-famous landscape architect Roberto Burle-Marx, who was designing the gardens, and Lucio Costa, who created Brasília's brilliant master plan. There were visits to other architects and to sites for carnival balls in preparation. The Bahiana dinners were delicious, the botanical gardens glorious, and the music enthralling. I recall Louis Armstrong being the only North American making enough sound for Brazilian ears. My only problem was attempting to keep pace with the quixotic moods of these people. They would be deeply concentrating on aspects of design when someone would suggest a coffee break. In minutes, they all would be making music and dancing on tables. My head spun!

With the artist Maria Bonomo, I visited the 1959 Biennale in São Paulo, then took off for Brasília. When our Viscount touched down in a cloud of red dust, I could barely discern a thin man in blue jeans grabbing my bag and making off with it. As I caught up with him, he suddenly turned to put out his hand. It was a smiling Oscar Niemeyer, architect of the whole city and, without doubt, a genius. His quarters were temporarily without water, so he was also staying in the new Palace Hotel. He would occasionally ask if I had time to talk. I saw Oscar's now legendary thumbnail sketches that went directly to the engineers as a means of fast-tracking the whole planning/building process. One day, as he and I walked down a new arcade, a ceiling tile fell, almost on our heads. I stopped while he strode on, saying, "Jack, *that* isn't architecture!" And so it was not. But how like his Biennale Palace in São Paulo, badly leaking and rusting out in its third year. We also argued about his vast office and housing blocks in Brasília, almost Miesian in their austere cubes of glass walls unshielded from the tropical sun. He claimed tinted glass would solve the heat buildup. I knew that even in our northern cities we resolved such heat gain only with powerful air-conditioning equipment, quite unaffordable there.

We also spoke about the fact that in off-hours his design team would head out to the construction workers' shantytown, not the pristine cafés just completed. I asked, "Can one breathe life into a city? Or have cities a life of their own, on which – as

Frank Lloyd Wright insists – the architect/city planner can only operate?" Oscar shrugged, "That may be, but it's fun to try."

When President Kubitschek's term soon ended, the southern Brazilian opposition party took over and building slowed. A coffee-crop failure bankrupted the country to the extent that even vital imports were unattainable, much less luxury fabrics for Brasília palaces. Ministers and bureaucrats happily ensconced in Rio were loath to move to the outback of Brasília, and the homestead plan was popular only with Japanese truck farmers. With the Brasília fabric program not going forward, I converted some of the design concepts for our 1960 Brazil Collection.

MEXICO

All through the late 1950s and early 1960s I spent part of each winter in Mexico, where my friends, Mane and Beach Riley, had a gracious home in San Angel. When I was not working on prints and weaves at the former studio of Jim Tillett, or handspun wools at the Riggs Sargent workshop, we toured the back country around Puebla and Taxco. As Beach was an avid sailor, we motored down to Acapulco to join his brother Lou and his wife, Dolores Del Rio. I sometimes envied Beach his "life of Riley." He and Lou, each with a million dollars, had come to Mexico in their twenties to own the first planes and to start the yacht club at Acapulco. Each had shared a carefree life with a succession of wives, keeping the best for last. Then one night, after much good wine, Beach lit into me as someone enjoying the pleasures of a career – something he had been deprived of.

I also worked on handwoven cotton cloths with Luis Rodriguez, a former taxi driver whose wife, Polly, was an American weaver from Arizona. When Polly ran off with a pig farmer, Luis raised the children and ran the handweaving studio. As he prospered Luis built a grandiose, three-story modern house for his boys. We would sit in his living room on fancy furniture covered with sheet plastic drinking Chivas Regal from Baccarat goblets.

Meanwhile, the American entrepreneur Olga de Campos bought the Jim Tillett shops on the Reforma and, with them, the handweaving and printing operation. Of good heart, she met with the weavers to say she was giving them the production facilities, including the building, equipment, and yarns. All she wanted from them was finished fabric for her shops. "Here is the Document of Transfer. Do you understand?" "Si, Señora."

From our Andean Collection, Conquistador interpreted a Baroque motif drawn by an Indian convert. The depth of coloring resulted from blocking a dense cotton velvet with hot wax, cracking the waxed cloth, dyeing it, removing the wax, and dyeing again.

That afternoon the weavers sold off the lot to the first takers! Rodriguez bought the silk screens, and with them the famous Tillett patterns I described at length in my book *The Dyer's Art*. Worse yet, government officials soon came to Olga saying she must pay out a year's wages "to the men she had discharged." Soon afterward, when our wool weaver, Wendell Riggs, died, our Mexican production dwindled.

SCANDINAVIA

My several early trips to Scandinavia played out in a lighter vein. For the first visit to Copenhagen, Sweden, and Helsinki, my friend Just Lunning, who owned Georg Jensen and bestowed the prestigious Lunning Prize, wrote letters of introduction the likes of which I have never seen since. In Copenhagen the manager of the posh Grand Bretagna gave me a suite with floor waiters hovering nearby. I had met the director of the Den Permante design emporium, who made the other introductions.

In Stockholm, Astrid Sampe and Ake Huldt treated me like a visiting movie star, with a full agenda and rounds of parties that made my head swim. As it was regatta time and the season for crayfish, we feasted and toasted so royally I finally fled to the guesthouse at Orrefors and the beautiful glass designer there, Ingeborg Lundin. After visiting a weaving mill in central Sweden for my Dux fabric assignment I returned to Stockholm for Marimekko's first opening outside of Finland. From across all the glowing color in the Artek Gallery a booming voice called, "Hey you, come over here. I want to talk to you. Yes, you with the funny hat!" It was Armi Rattia with Voulko Escolin, founders of Marimekko, who would return to Helsinki in time for my arrival.

The Finnish capital then was home to a dozen international designers at the height of their careers. I spent time with Dora Jung and Marjatta Metsovaara, Kaj Franck at Arabia, Tapio Wirkkala, the young Timo Sarpaneva, and Ake Tjeder, head of Artek and member of the Alvar Aalto office. As it was still summer, we were often treated to thin slices of reindeer meat served from a block of ice, and also steak tartare, here called *steak sauvage*. In Copenhagen it had been *steak cannibal*; by the time I reached Brussels for the great World's Fair of 1958, the term was *steak American*.

NEW ZEALAND

In 1974 I spent a fortnight in New Zealand for the International Wool Bureau. For me the trip was to make contact with upholstery and carpet weavers and to research the unknown wealth of Maori fabrics, principally structured of twined New Zealand flax or dog's hair. For the Wool Bureau it seemed an opportunity to parade an "expert" through all the cities and towns. On arrival in Auckland my plane was met by a host of reporters wanting an interview about my views on New Zealand. The weaver, Nan Berkeley, asked if I would lecture at the museum two nights later. On the night of the lecture, as we drove up to the substantial museum acropolis, I thought, "There will be a large auditorium; I hope they reached fifty by telephone to ensure an audience." There were six hundred, but in those days not a lot of competitive entertainment.

New Zealand, as it turned out, is the mirror image of America's West Coast, only upside down. Subtropical Auckland in the north is much like San Diego, hilly Wellington in the center like San Francisco. Cool, Scottish Dunedin, the southernmost city, felt like Vancouver, and the famous geysers reminded me of Yellowstone Park. Most of the tourists were also from the American West; to them it was just like home and they loved it. As my entourage motored to all of the cities and the towns between them, I was approached by their newscasters and television stations. If I could bring myself to say something bullish about the wool market, a headline would appear the next day – as bold as if war had been declared.

It was a beautiful country manicured by a hundred million animals to look like an endless country club. If the two and one-half million residents were proud of being egalitarian, I found the ubiquitous spartan four-room houses unromantic, and having only two waiters in a whole nation indicative of underprivilege. That the first settlements of the 1860s seemed to them ancient was also amusing. This was a beautiful land, full of potential.

One of my favorite parts of the trip was climbing trees in orchards abandoned for shortage of labor to pick undersized, overripe fruit with more flavor than I've found anywhere. The museums in every city were dominated by exhibits of South Pacific ethnography, including the considerable collections made by Captain Cook. For residents these unchanging galleries were a deprivation, but for the visitor, a bonanza. The photographer in my entourage took superb photographs in black-and-white and color of every piece I asked for.

As I flew across the Tasman Sea to Sydney and then all day over Australia's vast outback to Bali, I could not help but feel the immensity of the sparsely populated South Pacific. One could assume that all these places, so very far away, must be proximate to each other. They are not.

SOUTHEAST ASIA, VIA JAPAN

In the late fifties I was invited by the famous industrial designer Russel Wright to join his team for designing crafted exports in Taiwan and South Vietnam. Our three-year contract with the State Department meant my heading research into grass-weaving projects for both countries, including on-location work during the winter of 1959–60. My design assistant, Ruben Eshkanian, was to go over earlier and stay longer, aided by a corps of technicians and administrators.

By this date, there had been many such projects in the developing world, with – at best – mixed results. The most successful I knew of was by Cranbrook sculptor and former Rhodes Scholar John Risely, who developed capiz shell industries in the Philippines, a wide range of wooden wares, and basketry chairs. At the same time and place my weavemaster at Cranbrook, Marianne Strengell, designed all manner of fabrics with native materials, which, in the end, failed to find a market.

Although our team hoped to reach beyond these earlier experiences, we did not (at least in the short run) succeed. Because the dictators of both countries loudly opposed communism, their governments received princely sums of aid – 80 percent in cash and 20 percent toward improving productivity by creating jobs and viable exports, primarily those crafted at a preindustrial level. To the detriment of these projects, the recipient governments openly demonstrated an urge to subvert the program monies into short-term gains. We also learned that simple, rural people overtly and subconsciously resist change, finding it painfully unsettling to alter traditions rooted in seasonal activities, deep-seated values, and sometimes religion as well. In the end, it seemed that governments had much less chance for success than a few grassroots entrepreneurs committed to the long haul, using gut reaction and seat-of-the-pants solutions.

Still, what an adventure this turned out to be – a profound learning experience, certainly a departure from the small world I had known, and a lark! Phase I involved an intense immersion into the craft culture of both countries, utilizing the home

Near Saigon in 1960, Russel Wright and I worked with Madame du Kim's refugee weavers to produce mats and rugs woven with dyed sea grass.

movies Wright had made there. We analyzed materials available, simple production methods, and potential markets. Some history was available from old China hands advising us on how tradition had been in the thirties. Quantities of fiber arrived along with simple tools, including so-called tatami looms. Made for vertically strung, short, and widely spaced warps, this device was simply a heavy hardwood beam alternately pierced with a small hole and a three-inch slot across the width. By pulling the beam forward or back, the yarns in holes created a horizontal opening to insert a weft material. The weight of the beam was also useful in beating down the weft sufficiently to cover the warp, as in tapestry. Principally using dyed sisal and banana fiber, we wove samples for shaggy rugs that sparked a favorable response.

Forty years after the introduction of large jet planes, it is difficult to recall just how distant Southeast Asia used to be. I had known many visitors to China and Japan, some to India, and even a few who had, early on, touched down in Bangkok or Bali. The newly independent countries in between were still rural backwaters steeped in preindustrial traditions. Getting there was a long haul in 1959. I broke the trip with a stop in Honolulu to inspect a hotel our company was working on. The magnate Henry Kaiser had decided, nine months before his eightieth birthday, that he wanted the first hotel tower in the Pacific ready for that December celebration. When I arrived in October, flown-in steel was still rising at the top while the project of furnishing, including the installation of our printed fabrics, was finishing up on the lower floors. My conclusion was that a rich man could buy time, if dearly.

After a majestic hurricane, our plane took off for the thirty-six-hour flight to Tokyo. Stopping for fuel at Midway, Wake Island, and Guam, we learned how pivotal these island stations were. We also learned a lesson from a Korean nanny traveling with the family of a general. After departure, she braided her hair and changed into a kimono. At each eight-hour interval she emerged in a fresh one, while the rest of us became as travel-weary as our wrinkled, slept-in suits. There are people today who complain about twelve-hour flights from New York to Tokyo, but I am not one of them!

Greeted in Tokyo by former classmates Patricia and Dale Keller, my eyes opened to a new Japan. Bustling, smoggy, traffic-jammed and jerry-built, it was far different from the country I had learned about as a student in Seattle. I should add that Tokyo today is a wondrous city. The smog is gone. Streets are wider, with more trees. While seven layers of efficient subways have reduced surface traffic, decentralization has spread it out. The city now has many fine buildings by great Japanese architects.

Frank Lloyd Wright's 1912–23 Imperial Hotel appeared as if nothing had changed since the architect left. The menus and matchboxes his team had designed were the same; the dinnerware and etched glasses had been continuously renewed, as had the textured fabrics. The Prunier fish restaurant was still the best in Asia, the magical ballroom the largest. One day a familiar voice called across the lobby. It was Marianne Strengell returning from Manila with sad stories about the weave studios there, which never found a market niche. Weavers were disillusioned, and the metal loom parts were rusting.

Tokyo's great Takashimaya store was a revelation in its admixture of old and new, East and West. Decidedly new was the lofty cosmetics pavilion. At its center an immense torso of Santa Claus rose to the ceiling – with twenty lifesize blond, naked mannequins wriggling over this *papasan*'s corpulent body, tweaking and pinching. On an upper floor we found a large assemblage of doleful, prewar mannequins modeling wedding kimonos in black and persimmon. More to our liking was an area of counters with rolled kimono fabrics only thirteen inches wide but a dozen yards long. The least expensive, for commoners, were dull cottons mostly in deep indigo and very handsome. For a little more, small ikat patterns (*kasuri*) appeared on the same cloths. More ambitious ikat patterns cost more. Those with whitish grounds woven in Okinawa of banana fiber were coolly pristine and costly. Farther along were the colorful silks for young women. The best were fine tie-dyes (*shibori*). Others were embroidered over stencil-printed resists and paired with golden brocaded obi cloths.

Special salons were given over to the finest cloths, and the rest of these were brought out for inspection from a stockroom. When shopping with the daimyo princess Madame Araki I was shown minute ikat geometrics in brown and indigo recognizable as the symbolic turtle pattern. These "plain" dull kimono cloths – at ten thousand dollars – had much the same aesthetic as the simplest, ten-dollar ones. With my show of enthusiasm, they brought out a bolt of a similar cloth woven by a National Treasure and priced at eighty thousand dollars. To my untrained eye they were identical but I could imagine those who could distinguish the difference being, in a courtly society, "the few that mattered." Here, then, was the *shibui* understatement I knew in ceramics and screen painting.

Pat and I spent the rest of the day in the basement, which in those years was a thrift shop where Japanese could bring old goods to exchange for vouchers redeemable upstairs. Here were antique bowls and plates in stoneware and celadon, lacquer and enamel, which soon became mine, as did a prehistoric burial pot, lacquer champagne "glasses," and coin silver sake cups. Attendants brought us tea, then lunch. If the only bargain remaining in Japan today is used apparel (they do not wear hand-me-downs), the selection in those days was incredible. Dozens of kimonos, obis, and coats were packed up for us. I was advised to take a few with quilted silk padding to Taiwan, where "the house would assuredly be unheated." Today a number of these venerable garments are in the collection of the Brooklyn Museum.

When I arrived in Kyoto, I found an ancient city of narrow streets and two-story buildings, mostly gone now, but then quite untouched by the West or modernity. Or by time. Then the imperial villas were open to visitors who could contemplate each aspect of the rooms and gardens in the meditative manner intended, as opposed to the forty-five-minute forced march demanded today. Underdressed and stocking footed, in castles as cold as meat lockers, I felt transported to a most beautiful, perfected world. Stores then were stalls wide open to the street with only a small hibachi for warming hands. The *ryokan* was also cold. If only in the bath and under the futon the body warmed, no matter. One day I paid dearly to attend the kiln opening of a Living National Treasure but could not afford even a small pot. I had known the Japanese had more knowledge and taste than I; they already had deeper pockets.

HONG KONG

The Crown Colony was a small colonial city in 1959. Natty British officials oversaw customs and traffic still dominated by rickshas and handcarts. The Peninsula Hotel and the YMCA building towered above Kowloon, while two-story government buildings and a few mansions up Victoria Peak gave presence to Hong Kong Island. As for the rest, most was a rabbit warren of shop houses on narrow streets overwhelmed by drying laundry and tall banners promoting wares. Hard by the treeless mountains, the narrow landing strip received only small planes in daylight hours. The harbor estuary of the Pearl River was then

the soul of Hong Kong. Junks of all sizes with colorful pleated sails plied these waters, down to Macao and upriver to Canton. Houseboats and the sampans of fishers and shrimp netters scuttled between them and the dozens of freighters being loaded by lighters.

During the subsequent visits that winter I was pleased to have introductions to Jimmy Chen, the young tailor, and Ascot Chan, the old shirtmaker. I visited the father of Peter Yang, who had been at Cranbrook with me, and, notably, Charlotte Horstman, the antiquities dealer who then worked out of a small gallery on Ice House Street and her several mysterious "go-downs," Chinese warehouses filled with ancient treasures.

TAIWAN

A short flight brought us into the chilly smog of Taipei, where I stayed only long enough for formalities. I stopped at the new Grand Hotel, which Madame Chiang Kai-shek had tricked up with red paint to look like a Hollywood set. More impressive was the view from my window of young men doing drills with long staves. Their bodies were as well coordinated as fine machines, but their minds, trained to immediately react in unison to any command, were both awesome and frightening.

I recalled this chilling drill when, in 1973, I watched three-year-olds at the nursery school of a weaving mill near Canton. They were lined up in a spear-thrusting relay; the object of their attack was Madame Chiang! The four-year-olds sang for us in Cantonese, "The East Is Red"; the five-year-olds had graduated to "Taiwan Will Soon Be Ours!" In James Michener's *South Pacific* an officer muses, "How do people learn to hate? They are taught, so carefully taught, by the time they are six or seven or eight." These Chinese, it seemed, were starting much earlier.

Our station was not dreary Taipei but T'ai-chung, to the south and so sunny as to be the film center. At the edge of town, our headquarters was a Japanese-style compound quite adequate for the six Americans living there. Among the corps of weavers and others helping in research was my Taiwanese interpreter – who did not speak English! As he had long ago studied in France and remembered only slightly more French than I did, communication was perilous.

One of the challenges of our work in Taiwan was materials supply. As I scouted regional markets seeking possible fibers, I repeatedly found coils of wondrous stuffs that turned out to be fine translucent noodles. Other likely materials I purchased soon became a state monopoly, available only through government agents at triple the market price. We also battled against export taxes and other devices collectively known as the Chinese Squeeze. The clique of Mainland Chinese that had come over with Chiang Kai-shek seemed like a contingent of New Yorkers exiled in the Badlands of South Dakota and now trying to extort money from the local population. Eliciting American aid was a good start, but usury was even more lucrative. One hundred percent interest rates were usual, 10 percent a week not uncommon, and the Taiwanese were meticulous about paying obligations, even when further indebtedness was their only option. They were beginning to realize how well off they had been under Japan's progressive colonialism.

Many of our evenings were devoted to planning a grand Christmas party for the staff and their families, complete with gifts and an American-style buffet table. It was only then we learned that the girls who wove for us would not dine in public but, like squirrels, snatched food and then hid while eating it. On Christmas Eve we were rewarded by a group of Chinese Christians from a neighboring village who came to sing all the familiar carols in Taiwanese dialect.

When our New Year's Day came, I hired a driver to visit the old southern capital. Except for some ancient temples and shrines, now closed, it was not very interesting until I came upon a wedding celebration in a courtyard. As most of the group were playing instruments, I listened for a time, then was handed a triangle and invited to join in. After numerous giggles, cups of rice wine, and eye communications more meaningful than language, I was invited for supper in an adjoining hall. Before leaving, I rose to toast the newlyweds, thank the hosts, contribute to the dowry box, and say farewell – all in pidgin and a universal sign language I was rapidly learning.

SOUTH VIETNAM

The transfer to Saigon through Hong Kong was relatively easy. Our small core group there was headed by Nisei potter Ken Emurya and his Japanese wife. Jeep drivers and other personnel came from the U.S. Consulate. Saigon, a modern Eurasian city with broad, tree-lined boulevards laid out by the French in the 1920s, was exotic and leisurely and had an enviable winter climate. The women were remarkably beautiful. Ramrod thin, fair-skinned, and graceful in movement, they wore silky trousers under long-sleeved, fitted dresses, ankle-length but slit at the sides almost to the waist. A wide-brimmed straw hat tied under the chin, smart sunglasses, and a nifty bicycle completed the ensemble. Silent and aloof, they glided through rooms and enlivened the streets.

I became friends with one of them, Madame du Kim, who with her son headed an encampment of Catholic refugee weavers from Hanoi. She became responsible for the group when her husband and two other sons were killed as they rafted down the coast during the communist takeover. Although the weavers' facilities were primitive, particularly for dyeing, they understood producing for export and for money. Unlike most South Vietnamese, who were rice farmers bartering their surplus crop through middlemen, these northerners understood filling overseas orders and the need to make the samples to procure them. Together we wove sea grass into smooth, flat rugs with bold, horizontal stripes in rich colors much like the lush canvases Mark Rothko was painting in New York. For larger, heavier rugs we twisted sea grass into ropes to weave with tapestry joinings. As the warp was stretched on a horizontal frame just above the ground, any size could be woven. The largest, for a Saigon ballroom and half a block long, was amazing to watch in production.

Before traveling to South Vietnam I read *The Ugly American*, a novel about the seamy side of Saigon in the 1950s, when the opium dens were still open and the American element was composed of rank opportunists. By 1960 Saigon was considerably cleaned up, probably to help win United States support. I found no iniquity but only well-meaning Americans bent on making improvements. Their wives volunteered as teachers and nurses' aides. Even so, Americans were not popular. The French had invited the local gentry to their parties; the Americans mistakenly did not. Our diplomats returned home before their replacements arrived, so each contingent was as innocent as the last.

I made friends with the U.S. Department of Agriculture team that was bringing about the hugely successful Green Rice project. Also working in Taiwan and South Vietnam, they experienced difficulties similar to mine. Due to a tradition of planting last year's rice after it had been blessed, finding any farmers willing to plant other rice, even if it would double the yield, seemed impossible. They finally identified a farmer willing to accept their gift. When the Yanks came back to see how he was doing, they found only half of his paddies planted. Less work was acceptable; change was not. An offer of huge, modern fishing nets was also turned down with the explanation that fish were now such a luxury that fishermen had status; if fish became plentiful, their social position would diminish!

My big assignment was a field trip to central Vietnam. Alone except for a trusted, well-armed jeep driver familiar with this war-torn area, my mission was to meet with silk weavers near the ancient capital of Hue. We had not gone far when a tower of smoke signaled a Viet Cong blockade of burning trucks. Without even showing alarm, my driver veered off the road into a burned-out jungle. As we forged streams and circled thickets, I was less concerned about snipers and land mines than the tigers who prowled this terrain.

Finally back on the road again, we called on fish-oil workers near the sea. Making fish oil (a Vietnamese food staple and often their only source of animal protein) was considered a handcraft; I was to inspect production. As all seemed in order, we went on to an encampment of northern refugees making rice cakes, another "handcraft." These large translucent sheets, resembling animal skins drying in the sun, were covered with flies. The children were so fly-bitten they had running sores. I told the lay priest in charge of the camp that if they could not find some cheesecloth to cover the rice cakes, I would send some. He expressed surprise, then conferred with his colleagues. Their response to my offer was, "Vietnam is a rice bowl, with enough rice for both flies and people!"

After ferrying two rivers under bombed-out bridges, we finally came to Hue. It was an impressive city of substantial old buildings ringing a bay dotted with small islands. The local command hosted a fine dinner, which included the delicacy of birds' eggs gathered by monkeys trained to raid nests on the island's cliffs. The next day, as we set off for the silk-weaving villages, there were more bridges down. The first river mouth we ferried on a sampan. At the second we transferred gear into a small boat, then picked up a vehicle on the far side. As we neared our destination in the late afternoon, I looked over my notes. The silk I was seeking was honan, the fine, handwoven tussah cloth most desired by fashion designers in Paris and New York. Before the war it had been woven in both China and central Vietnam. With China closed to the West, this trade could be a bonanza for the new republic.

Our purpose was obviously well known, as the headmen were waiting to take us on a torch-lit tour of the loom sheds. I saw storage areas crammed with peculiar, pattern-making drums not seen before or since. In the manner of a player piano, pegs on these drums created small patterns in the cloth. The villagers' enthusiasm was heartening. They could still weave and some had been renowned for their skill. I was thrilled with their eagerness to revive this ancient tradition. A big advantage was that while it would take years to restore mulberry plantations and cultivate silkworms for normal sericulture, tussah yarn for honan cloth is produced from the collected cocoons of wild moths. Production could soon be under way.

Trouble began during negotiations the next morning. It turned out that what they were keen to weave was not silk but cotton uniform cloth for their newly liberated country. In this hot climate, uniforms were made of the thin cotton camouflage cloth printed in Japan for about ten cents a yard. I came up with a solution: "For each yard of silk produced, you will receive forty yards of uniform cloth to give your country." The answer was, "No! We will be wasting our time working for foreigners we will never meet." "But," I reasoned, "your country also needs money for exchange." "No" again, and "Tell the blond American that we have money, it comes from foreign aid!" That was it; no amount of negotiating would alter the impasse.

Thinking that perhaps the Diem dictatorship could order honan production, we retreated back across flooded river mouths toward Saigon. The route this time was west of hostilities, through the highlands to Da Lat. This region has sufficient altitude to provide the coast with temperate-zone fruits and vegetables. In the old days Da Lat also offered French colonials respite from Saigon's steamy summers. Now in winter and with the French gone, the hotels, parks, and deserted streets had taken on the semblance of a silent Surrealist film with but a solitary figure in view: mine.

Russel Wright paid a visit soon after my return to Saigon. Since my arrival in Taiwan, his communications had been cryptic cables airing his frustration with bureaucratic obstacles he could not comprehend in New York. When upset by Russel's impatience, I would listen to my favorite recordings of Carl Sandburg, reading with the same Hoosier accent as Russel's! Now we faced a real problem with the mill weavers' request for our help. The Diem regime had reinstated the French colonial tariff system. This meant no duty on cloth imports but high duties on yarns and manufacturing equipment, including that

Jim Thompson, Thailand's legendary Silk King, was particularly helpful during my 1960 sojourn in Southeast Asia. He is seated here on a Thai bed in his famous art-filled house on the Klong, which he originally showed me as five separate houses along the river.

coming in as foreign aid. In protest, the mill workers marched on the capital, only to be told that as soon as they could supply all the country's textile needs, the tariff laws would change.

Reasonably incensed by the injustice of this impasse, Wright commanded Diem to meet in our office at ten o'clock on Sunday – the exact hour of the fashionable mass that Diem attended. On his arrival, Russel waived the expected cordiality, saying only, "Please sit down." He first reminded the embarrassed president that our team represented the U.S. State Department. Then he read him the riot act, with a long list of reforms to be signed that morning, including changes in textile tariffs. Under such direct attack, Diem capitulated without protest. Although this sudden victory was probably a brief one, I congratulated Russel as I saw him off to Phnom Penh. My own departure for Cambodia and Angkor Wat was on the next weekly plane. Dozens of Vietnamese we were working with came to the airport, including Madame du Kim and her weavers, all carrying gifts and flowers. When my plane neither arrived nor departed, there was nothing to do but pretend it had. I accepted their farewells, then came back into the city incognito.

THAILAND AND BURMA

While in Vietnam, I had spent most weekends in Bangkok with Jim Thompson, the legendary American entrepreneur who revived silk weaving there at the close of World War II. He managed to bring in silk warp yarns from Japan and local silk from up-country, then found Muslim weavers to reel, dye, and weave for him. These silks, in dazzling arrays of iridescent colors often sparked with Siamese pink, found a following in part because of Jim's extraordinary marketing skills.

Trained as an architect, tall, ash-blond, and congenial, Jim was toastmaster of the expatriate community and a host to increasing numbers of American and European visitors. Single, with ample staff and a growing collection of Thai and Burmese art, he frequently gave dinners for these travelers, few of whom have forgotten the experience. The next day he would supervise their silk selections for dressmaking and decorating back home. I marveled at the charm of his sales pitch: "Well, good morning! I've been waiting for you as I need advice. It's about this silk cloth . . . isn't it marvelous how the folds catch the light? When Queen Elizabeth ordered some I promised to keep it exclusive. Then, the Princess of Paris pleaded to have a large yardage . . . she is so beautiful, how could I turn her down? Now I have a cable from Marlene Dietrich asking for the same pattern!

What? You want some too? Pretty lady, you are not helping my dilemma at all!"

Jim's overseas demand swelled after Irene Sharaff used these glowing silks for costuming various companies of *The King and I*. When he was asked to weave rustic, matte-surfaced cloths for costumes for a new version of the film *Ben-Hur*, Thompson developed the heavy, all-Thai silk cloth we know as Shan. Some days I joined Jim touring the weaving compounds. Other times he sent me off with a young monk to see the wonders of Siam. One particularly fine day Jim and I cruised through the back canals to measure the five old houses he was considering joining together for his now-famous House on the Klong. As the teak-wood posts and panels of Thai houses were built to be moved when river courses changed, it would be an easy transformation.

He also loaned me books tracing the evolution of Buddhist sculpture from its Grecian beginnings at Gandhara, through India to Southeast Asia, China, and Japan. His books and my long reflections on the magnificent Buddhist bronzes in the National Museum gave me a level of appreciation not replicable in my short visits of recent years. That, it seemed, was the point. In not valuing time or money, this corner of the world was then totally different. I realized that Europe, America, and Japan were bound together by the realities of time. South Asia did not measure time as linear progression, but accepted it as vague and multilayered. In this more serene world, I enjoyed a brief respite from the overwhelming drive for achievement. Perhaps sensing this, Jim encouraged me to consider staying on to be "the Jim Thompson of Burma."

When my Saigon stint ended, I took his introductions and a two-engine plane to Rangoon. That old settlement at the mouth of the Irrawaddy River was a weaver's paradise. Everyone still wore *longi* tube skirts, handwoven in the broadest array of weaves I had yet seen, an amalgam of all the skills and traditions of Europe and India. They also wove brocades, tapestries, lampas, ikats, and textured handspuns in several weaves not used elsewhere. Businessmen wearing hard-finished silk taffetas and moires by day changed into looser, more voluptuous *longis* for evening. Sheer shirtings fastened by silver or gold studs with chains were worn under short, snug-fitting jackets. Small straw caps swathed in crisp ecru organza gave their diminutive wearers the look of quizzical cockatoos. Then as now, the bands of Buddhist monks wore robes and blankets in orchestrations of earthy oranges, ranging from amber to coral and henna. At night, classic Burmese opera was performed in the open air.

Back in Mandalay twenty years after my first visit in 1960, I found only the temples unchanged. Two decades of stringent communism had wiped out a gracious, peaceful culture and, with it, a dynamic textile heritage embracing many techniques of Indian and European origin.

Near Chiang Rai in northern Thailand, I am demonstrating an alternative weaving method for hill-tribe weavers. As in most of Southeast Asia, weaving here takes place in the shade, under houses raised on stilts.

At intermission, the same performers played slapstick with all the familiar pratfalls and head-beating we know in the West.

The combination of Burmese, Chinese, and South Indian traders made Rangoon a fascinating melting pot bathed in an aura of British colonialism. Best of all were remnants everywhere of the Burmese love of ornament fused with Victorian taste for the overblown. These two cultures had been on the same wavelength, reveling in a heady effusiveness that was visible in bandstands and cast-iron market buildings, carved black furniture, richly worked embroideries, and beaded lampshades. In closed parlors this would have been much too much, but in open loggias it was enchanting.

I had liked South Burma, but Mandalay was a dream. Although the Lacquer Palace had burned, the great temples and their cloistered markets remained a hubbub of boisterous activity. The U.S. Information Service loaned me a jeep and driver to tour nearby villages and the national weaving school. I visited famous weavers whose looms were tightly covered with pinned muslin. As dress styles never changed, these weavers were couturiers and their new cloths well-guarded secrets.

In Rangoon I had met with the Minister of Industry. His questions concentrated on whether I was a worker or only an expert. Experts were being deported, including good teams from the Ford and Asia Foundations, while technicians from Eastern Europe were considered workers. He was also suspicious of the number of Burmese cloths I had purchased but, in the end, welcomed my coming back to work with his people, the weavers.

I had cabled Win and Manning that I would be back in the United States for a few months to wind up my affairs, then move to Burma. Fortunately, the windup and addressing new challenges took longer than expected; soon Burma was closed to the world outside and became a repressive communist state. At best, I might have been jailed for twenty years.

As is so well documented in Bill Warren's book *The Legendary American,* Jim Thompson disappeared while on holiday with friends in 1967. Although there was speculation of his having been kidnapped to China or Cambodia, the mystery is still unsolved. Connie Mangskau, who was with him at the time, told me that she felt Thompson was done in immediately, but she had no clue as to why or by whom. For years servants at the house expected his return, but his firm, the Thai Silk Company, needed some resolution. Business continued with Charles Sheffield as managing director but, as design development was

Jim's province, the line was stagnant; especially overseas business slipped away. In America the distributing firm, Thaibok, languished because taste for dazzling color was now over, and Jim's old designs became dated.

In 1971 George Barrie, who had the largest number of Thai Silk Company shares, approached me to design for them. "Only if we can buy the North American distribution," I answered. And so our company bought Thaibok Ltd., the firm I had worked with twenty years earlier and with which I had sought to merge. I began a series of long trips to work in the weave sheds of Thailand. Jim had been an architect and a fine colorist, but he was not a weaver. Keen to design in areas he had not, I began the first innovations in what became an industrial revolution.

As the Siamese traditionally used only plain weave, Jim had accepted this limitation. Although changing from two to four harnesses to weave twills and simple brocades at first seemed overwhelming, one weaving group accepted my challenge to work with luscious long floats of creamy silk. To make a durable upholstery I added polyester sewing thread to the warp for the herringbone twill of our Silk Canvas. Even more fun was starting up the first production ikats where the weft yarn is wrapped to a prescribed pattern so as to resist dye. Over a Christmas holiday at Round House I tore greeting cards into a collage design. When I went back to Bangkok on Valentine's Day, the up-country ikat weaver drove down with successful samples. My torn paper was so much like the feathered edges of ikat that her translation was remarkably close. While indigenous ikats were woven in short lengths as skirt cloths, our bolts were forty yards long in heavy upholstery weights.

This was my first project with Bill Booth, a young American who had learned Thai and the countryside, then joined the company. With him and my former student Geraldine Scalone, we explored northern Thailand and the nomadic hill tribes there. We also developed new screenprints over color-woven silk grounds. Although they could already print with a bleaching agent mixed with a dye to discharge out the ground color – a sophisticated process that has a fine craft quality – the finishing was achieved with heavy clothes irons heated with charcoal.

Our first Thai Silk Collection was launched at Lord & Taylor as a homage to Jim Thompson. When we introduced these exotics in Europe I showed the blossom-hued cloths to my friend Andrée Putman. She was standing tall in ecru crepe,

Bill Booth, Geraldine Scalone, and I researched hill-tribe craftmakers on the northern Thai frontier, where the Karen women were wary of our cameras.

Opposite, top: In Khorat, in northeastern Thailand, Bill Booth is translating to Kun Ratri my design for a revolutionary new ikat design.

Opposite, bottom: Because I am using as weft six heavy silk strands as one yarn instead of one fine strand, I have asked them to wrap the resist with plastic ribbon instead of cotton thread.

Left: The resulting heavy upholstery fabric, Laotian Ikat, is woven in forty-yard bolts, not the traditional two-yard tube-skirt length. Its feathered pattern closely resembles a collage I designed with torn paper.

Below: Another colorway of Laotian Ikat is shown here with my other silk ikats, as well as fabrics and a Wilton carpet inspired by ikat patterns.

My recent designs for Thai Silk are often as anonymous as these, the first satins woven there. The dense structure in fine yarns permits a cloth reversing from red to green (center), with green shadows in the red cloth and vice versa.

without discernible makeup and only ivory and jet jewelry. Her response was, "Jacques, don't you know that color is *over*?" As I thought about this, even our next Thai Silk cloths neutralized. My next collection, Crystal Palace, was without color or texture, and America went into its first beige decade. Years later, when I was seated next to Andrée at a dinner at the Museum of Modern Art, I warned her, "Color is back!" She responded, "Yes, Jack, and it is black!"

Over the years of returning to Bangkok to work on new designs at Thai Silk Company, I witnessed an entire revolution in production. The first change was having most weavers work in one company-owned production studio. Their move up to northeastern Thailand ended with a vast tree-shaded campus of weave sheds and dyehouses. Recent additions there are modern spinning systems and power looms, printing machines in a modern finishing plant, and a silk farm for sericulture. All this was achieved without losing the handcraft potentials I have employed in recent designs. Better yet, the weavers can still bicycle to the campus from nearby villages to have steady work without moving into a metropolitan slum.

Gerald Pierce, whom I brought to Bangkok to work on our Larsen World Collection, stayed on to become the leading designer in Thailand. With Bill Booth he has resurrected the Jim Thompson name with great success, including fine innovations and complex weave structures. I would give anything to come back with Jim Thompson to see these wonders.

KOREA

Even before returning to Thailand I met in our New York studio Chinsoo Paek, a young Korean working with an American team in Seoul to develop handcrafts for export. When he showed me their imitation of a Jim Thompson plaid, I asked, "Why do you want to take business from another poor country? Why not make fabrics not done by others, such as warp prints?" I explained that by printing the warps before weaving they would achieve the craft quality of ikats. Soon Leslie Tillett, the creative Anglo-American who had performed such wonders in Mexico, was in Korea improvising an ingenious way of producing these fabrics. By the time I started working with Paek the mechanics were resolved. Our contribution was only to combine warp printing with more complex structures. The speed and efficiency with which these weavers produce still amaze us. Sometimes a sample is back within a week. In the countryside farmers run where others would walk. Although the whole area around Seoul has developed even faster than Southeast Asia – the former wilderness area near the weave studios is now built up with condominiums – the progress is more agreeable and road traffic somewhat more tolerable. The new museum buildings and a symphony hall are world-class, but the best diversion remains the National Museum. Its historical rooms and galleries of Korean ceramics from the Koryo and Silla dynasties are peerless. A consolation for my visits – invariably in winter – is the spectacle of persimmon trees everywhere, leafless to better ripen a myriad of large red fruit.

JAPAN

Japan continues to be my favorite country. I am there at least once a year, sometimes twice. My headquarters used to be Kyoto, to focus on traditional Japan. When Osaka built an international airport, I could fly there and taxi to the Tarawaya Ryokan in an old section of Kyoto. The bullet train would speed short trips for business in Tokyo or Nagoya. But with the yen climbing in value, I was pleased not to be producing textiles in Japan. The porcelain factories in Nagoya, which manufactured my dinnerware for Dansk and Mikasa, were so efficient as to weather the exchange. Faster than in other countries, automation aided all phases of production. For my Tapestries service for Dansk, when the original pressings achieved only 30 percent first quality, we were asked to design patterned decals to disguise flaws. Fortunately, a robot was soon pressing perfect wares. It is called "robotic assist," but in fact the potter assists the robot. Old Kyoto, of course, is still there, with many craftsmakers in all disciplines, but I find depressing the invading commercialism.

Tokyo, in the meantime, is reinventing itself as a vertical city divided into far-flung centers. Broader streets and raised expressways speed surface traffic, while most people move through a labyrinth of immaculate, efficient subways underground. Pollution is gone and trees have been planted, but better yet is the spirit of optimism. Most of the people I meet there expect life to become better.

That is just the point. One hundred years ago America was so eager to catch up with Europe that we passed it by to invent mass production and department stores, modern communications, Hollywood, and popular cars. Today East Asia, but particularly Japan, is in that same position. And it comes quickly. Phone cords disappeared there a decade ago. Cold beverages

One of the several Japanese craftsmakers I met who had been designated a National Living Treasure, Fukumi Shimura of Kyoto was by far the youngest and most accomplished. The range of beauty of her kimonos, using only plain weave, reminds me of the quiet perfection of Morris Graves's flower paintings.

Like their international coterie of friends and colleagues, I have been enriched by the longtime friendship of Issey Miyake and his fabric designer, Mikiko Minagawa. As optimists and workaholics, we three share many passions.

A house front in northern Nigeria reveals the long-standing tradition of painted symbols, old and new.

have long been sold in bags with a straw. When I lived in Taiwan decades ago I saw firsthand the transition from selling fresh meat with only a banana-leaf finger holder to carry it home to using thin plastic bags for every purpose. The phase of paper wrapping had been bypassed completely.

More importantly, thought races forward. The optimum is not dismissed as an impossibility. Superb quality is still a norm. Then, too, Asian achievers travel and observe to become more cosmopolitan, perhaps because they escape the parochial limits of New Yorkers or Parisians thinking they are at the center.

I am happy to be working in contemporary Japan, on the cutting edge of new developments in both woven and printed fabrics. The yen is still high, but Japanese efficiencies have kept prices at an affordable level. We have an easy, trusting give-and-take. It's as if I ask, "Having achieved the difficult, can we now try the impossible?" Their eyes open wide, air is inhaled quickly through clenched teeth, knuckles whiten, and then, looking up, their response is, "We will try." That's enough. For these are people who deliver better than promised.

WEST AFRICA

In Alberta for my twelfth summer, I watched a documentary film on Princess Elizabeth's tour of the West African colonies. What impressed me most were the wondrous houses in the background. Some looked like great beehives built of clay, others were round wooden structures grouped in a circle, and still others resembled thick-walled, enormous sand castles gleaming against the dusty desert backdrop. "When I grow up," I thought, "I will visit those buildings and the amazing black-skinned people who make them."

And I did! In the summer of 1960 we had a long visit from Arthur Goldreich, a good client from Johannesburg. When Arthur invited me to visit him, I responded that my interest was in West Africa. "That settles it," he said. "Nigeria is the largest and most important of the new West African nations. My classmate, Dr. Tim Gordon, has already spent two years there, knows the country, and could arrange your trip, en route to South Africa."

My colleague Win Anderson agreed to join me. We traveled first to Cologne and Frankfurt to survey production for Larsen Europe, then left Zurich with the first snowfall to cross the Sahara into steamy Lagos on the Bight of Benin. Since I had worked in Haiti and Brazil, tropical slums and poverty were not new to me. Lagos was worse, without any alleviating charm.

Creoles have style, music, a merry gait, and exotic cuisine – all absent there. Attempts to incorporate indigenous carving skills into the few prominent buildings were without grace. There was one pleasant dinner on a veranda facing the sea, but at 10 P.M. the breeze stopped, the heat and mosquitoes moved in, and we retreated to screened bedrooms.

At the University in Ibadan we encountered Tim Gordon, who had ready a complete itinerary of field trips for the central kingdoms and the northern Sudan. With him we visited the Ibo peoples and the Ife with their famous courtyard of bronze heads marked with parallel furrows of vertical scarification. We toured the old palaces at Benin and caught the spectacle of a Yoruba priestess dancing in ecstasy. Like other former colonies rimming the Gulf of Guinea, Nigeria is layered into a humid Christian belt along the sea, a forested pagan area producing most of the carved masks, and an arid north populated by Muslim peoples.

It was in the forested region that we found most of the architecture I wanted to see. Like most young Africans, a man here works hard to earn bride wealth. Once married, the couple builds a house and farm, working from dawn until dark to earn money for a second wife, then the three of them work toward a third. The wives then farm while the man retires to the men's council. As each wife has a small round house and initiated sons even smaller ones, plus the granaries and walled animal pens, a household becomes a village replete with usable spaces between buildings, some of them shaded from the brutal sun. Whether built of wood, reeds, or clay, these compounds are more intriguing than monolithic houses.

Then even less known than West African architecture was the richness of the fabric traditions. Win and I were astounded by the variety of cloths in the so-called blue markets, with resist patterns worked by women and indigo dyed by men. There were tie-dyes of many types including bold and fine-scaled fold-dyed cloths in both vertical bands and concentric panels. Stitch resists allowed a broad range of imagery, while batiks of casaba starch resist were both freely drawn and stenciled onto cotton sheeting. The results were splendid, as was the style with which these free-spirited people wore garments as simple as two sheets joined at the shoulders. At the time of our visit (just after independence), there were many celebrations of indigenous music, dance, and costume. Craftmakers were also having a heyday.

The so-called blue market in Ibadan teems with indigo resists created by fold-dyeing or stenciling casaba paste onto the cotton cloth before dyeing.

Freely translating the fabric wealth of Nigeria's blue markets, Tony Ballatore drew Tropic of Capricorn for our Africa II Collection. Screenprinted on a dense cotton cloth, it proved to be as durable as it was glamorous.

Like Timbuktu, but connected to an agrarian support system, Kano is a caravan terminus. Camel trains still carried in trade goods from across the Sahara. Whether the leather slippers, scratchy wool blankets, and strands of beads in the markets came from Tunisia, Morocco, or Upper Volta was hard to guess. Kano was also the rail terminus. Near the sidings were giant pyramids of bagged groundnuts: peanuts destined for oil extraction and export, but also a local food staple, especially in groundnut soup, which can be as tasty as it is nutritious.

The Hausa men of Kano wore cut-and-sewn djellabas gowns of mill-woven shirting, pointed leather slippers, and embroidered pillbox hats. For ceremonial wear, they put on heavy robes of handspun, strip-woven cotton, most often in indigo or natural, and lavishly emblazoned with Islamic symbols by men working feverishly on foot-treadle sewing machines. Even more rewarding were our visits to weaving compounds where narrow looms were lined up under long sheds open on one side to a courtyard of raked sand. Lengthy warps only six inches wide were wound into a bundle, then placed under a weight on a small sled in the courtyard. As the men wove, the sleds were slowly pulled across the sand. The striped warps were horizontally banded with areas of simple brocading. Unlike the clack-clacking of flying shuttle looms in South Asia, these were silent. So were the solemnly focused weavers, in contrast to the matronly weavers of "women's cloth," who chatted merrily while repeatedly forming openings to push through the handspun wefts on their vertical looms.

We also visited indigo dye vats set into the ground out on the plain. The cold dye liquor was intermittently stirred until the wetted cloth was almost black. Then it was spread out to dry before being beaten smooth with a paddle. Without rinsing, the indigo was fugitive: excess dye rubbed off easily, but having blue-brown skin was proof of wearing authentic indigo. We viewed a darkened shed of men seated around a great bolt of folded mill cotton, rhythmically beating indigo into it until the cloth was as weighted and glossy as carbon paper. Later we saw policemen proudly wearing it as stiffly belled military shorts above their blued knees.

Although the rounded blackware pots of the Yoruba were distinguished, those of the Sudan were interesting only for their utility. We witnessed their production in the open air and without a potter's wheel. Working on the ground and bent over double, a tall man running in a circle formed clay hemispheres between his hands. Instead of using clay water as the lubricant,

he added clay dust as a baker sprinkles flour onto loaves. The bowl formed, he placed it upside down over an old pot and continued circling the pot until a volumetric, wide-mouthed vessel was complete. When leather-hard, these pots were simply ornamented with engraved lines, sun dried, and fired on the open ground.

Most attractive of the peoples in the Sudan, the light-skinned Fulani are a seminomadic group with the aquiline features of Nubians and the grace of antelopes. After a long drive across the parched Sudan, we reached a Fulani village on the day of a "beating." The beating, it turned out, was the final phase of the adolescent boys' initiation, a test of their courage in not succumbing to pain. This we did not see, but were cordially entertained by a handsome young prince whose hair was braided, then wrapped in pure gold to fall by his face like the eagle feather of American Indian braves.

On a journey south into wooded country, our guesthouse was a row of tents. I had just seen Win to her tent and found my bed in the darkness next door when her scream pierced the night. Imagining a panther with its head in her tent, I grabbed a pole and rushed to the rescue. There was no panther; instead, only an apple-sized spider hanging over her bed! As Win had hunted rattlesnakes in Montana but was phobic about spiders, my rescue was easily done. The next day before noon we reached our destination, a Ubangi settlement. Here was a whole village of people unadorned except for circular lips protruding up to ten inches! This did not tempt our cameras, but small twin girls – still untouched – invited us to photograph them. When they posed, then giggled and ran away, I assumed it might be to find a leaf to cover their nudity. But no, they returned smiling and "dressed" with small ivory lip plugs.

Our last and longest drive, toward Lake Chad in the east, was to visit an emir. Along the way our driver kept picking up a relay of young interpreters, each knowing the language of the people just beyond. Built of reeds, the emir's village was impressive and scrupulously swept, but apparently empty until someone pointed to the large Council House.

We entered a tall circular room that seemed dark. Coming out of the blazing sun, we barely discerned the enthroned emir surrounded by elders seated on an earthen curb. When their interpreter explained our quest, then brought a simple high stool, Win gratefully sat down. Silently but quickly four men raised the stool and, with it, carried her out! Women were not allowed in the Council House; for one to sit higher than the emir was scandalous. The day was saved when scribes noticed our cameras: would we please photograph His Excellency? And so, we spent the afternoon recording his presence while bearers brought out changes of jewelry displayed on cushions, then a succession of robes and headdresses, and finally his prize stallions.

The return trip was uneventful. Win retired. I went to a club outdoors lighted by open fires and dined with a gentle merchant from Khartoum. Some jolly young women who knew the Lindy but preferred the new African steps taught me to dance the High Life. The next morning, while we waited for the plane to Johannesburg, I was arguing about an excess baggage fee larger than the airfare when a Lebanese trader approached. He asked, "Will you give me the pleasure of paying this small bill? All I do out here is make money, and there is nothing here to spend it on!"

SOUTH AFRICA

How exciting to be in South Africa! One of the richest and most beautiful countries in the world, it was, in the early 1960s, secretly poised for revolution. South Africa is as verdant as a sun-filled California unspoiled by man. Where Americans might have put up billboards, South Africans built another park with benches designated for "Europeans," "Asians," and "Africans," to stratify populations of three, one, and twenty-one million, respectively. There were, as well, a few hundred thousand "coloreds" resulting from admixtures of Africans and early French colonists.

And what a happy land! The Europeans were blithely building hundred-room houses that had elsewhere become white elephants. The former Asian laborers, now middle-class, worked to educate children beyond their station. The Africans were smiling, too, when observed. After coming from Nigeria, where the only Europeans remaining were indispensable engineers and scientists, it seemed strange to see white elevator operators and store clerks.

En route to his farm outside Johannesburg, Arthur Goldreich began to explain what we would not see. The new government was even more reactionary than the previous one. As liberal-minded residents with British passports had to become South African citizens or emigrate, most were leaving, many for California. When the Asians were offered European status as a ploy to strengthen the white minority, they declined. The Afrikaner descendants of the Dutch Boers were determined to keep power; the Africans were too restricted, too spread out to easily take over the country, and too well guarded. The secret service was better organized than the former German Gestapo, with informers planted in every corner. Even peaceful protests such as sitting down in the face of the grossest indignities were met with tanks and machine-gun fire.

Arthur Goldreich – an architect, artist, scion of Johannesburg's founding fathers, wartime major, and a hero in the Battle of Jerusalem – was now deeply committed to the cause of equality. For the sake of privacy he moved from Johannesburg to his farm, where the African opposition leader, Nelson Mandela, was hiding in a swamp. We met him after dark, over dinners. While Goldreich's magnetism was overt, Mandela's ran deep, under a gentle, wary facade. After our departure, when Nelson was imprisoned, Arthur became the leader of the opposition. Consequently the Goldreich family and everyone else at the farm were jailed without trial. After Arthur escaped and narrowly missed three assassination attempts, he moved to Israel to become a leader in pro-Palestinian relations.

Our visit to the Transvaal included meeting a Swazi dealer in carved bowls and the extraordinary handspun, handwoven drapery cloths by Coral Stephens. These are among the most beautiful and costly fabrics woven today, unique in their translucence and superb draping quality. After their introduction as a small group in my African Collection, they became top-of-the-line fabrics in both our American and European showrooms. When I was later commissioned to design the stage curtain at the Wolf Trap Theater, I chose Coral Stephens as the producer. On opening night the King of Swaziland and I sat in the presidential box; the fabric was the largest Swazi export.

One day we set out early for the N'debele village now famous for walls painted by women in monochromes or brilliant primary colors sparked with white and black. As Arthur had once spent a summer there and knew the young N'debele prince we were shown the houses and his beaded treasures. Perhaps an offshoot of the Zulu, the monogamous N'debele families live side-by-side in villages and work in fields some distance away. Within the walled rowhouse plots, the zones are distinct for each family member. Out front stand all manner of lavishly painted masonry structures where women sit during evening hours watching their children at play. Just behind is a commodious, swept courtyard where the husband entertains friends in the shade of peach trees. Next stands his circular house, built across the full width of the yard. In back of this is a courtyard and rectangular house for women and children.

It was the man's house that excited me. As the central room was wrapped only halfway around with auxiliary spaces, windows (and potentially doors) to the outside were possible. Postwar American and European architects had been intrigued with circular plans, but invariably divided the circle into pie-shaped rooms, disturbing in themselves and impossible to furnish with rectangular beds and storage units. In his Endless House concept, Frederick Keistler reminded us that the eye perceives space by "measuring it corner to corner." This round room would retain a degree of infinity while the smaller rooms ringing it would have the straight walls of the radius plus usable segments parallel to the outer circumference. The conical roof had its own appeal. My mind was spinning! On a trip through the great animal preserves of Kruger Park I drew circular house plans at night. By the time we reached the highlands of Zulu-land, I was cutting out brown paper models by torchlight. (See Round House aerial view, page 94.)

The animals of Africa intrigued us much more than expected. In South Africa and later in Kenya, their enormous numbers and the power of the herds impressed us with a majesty unimaginable in zoos and circuses. Seeing cars flattened like beer cans by ill-tempered elephants spoke of a brute strength. The speed of running giraffes, the variety of stripes in zebra herds, the thunder of stampeding wildebeests, the indolent sloth of wallowing hippos were all fascinating. One morning we closely followed grazing white rhinos, and in the afternoon herds of the black rhinoceros, reputed to be extremely dangerous. Although nearsighted, their sense of smell is keen. Suddenly aware of Win, who was out front, they charged with the speed and force of a panzer division! From a distance I could see our white hunter and the beaters scaling trees. Paralyzed with terror, Win was not even running fast! When the wind changed and the rhino charge ended in a disgruntled rout, our men rushed to her defense.

The tall, stately Zulus impressed us with their somber, melancholy grace. The ones who live in rocky highlands built fortresslike structures, more to protect against marauding animals than enemy attack. Much more to our liking than Zululand was Durban. There Zulu youths migrate to town to earn bride wealth as ricksha boys. Their earnings go into beaded amulets, breast plates, bracelets, and incredible swaying head-

dresses that increase their impressive height to over ten feet. To see all of this moving through the streets on such prime, coordinated bodies was like ballet.

AFGHANISTAN

The urge to visit West Africa came to me when I was twelve, to visit Japan and the Orient at nineteen. The need to know something of the heartland of Central Asia developed later and at a deeper level; it festers still. Will I ever comprehend this great fountainhead of migrating peoples, erupting as thundering hordes since the dawn of time? What compelled these waves of invaders to move out of the steppes and barren mountains – the Celts, Aryans, Dorians and Ionians, Scythians, Mongols, Turks and Ottomans, Finns and Magyars? Moving to greener pastures is comprehensible, but to repeatedly take over so much of Eurasia requires explanation. Their vigor fascinates me; so does the remarkable strength of the arts they generated. I have always felt such tribal styles to be closer to the lifestyle of red-blooded Americans than are the courtly traditions of Renaissance Europe.

A conversation many years ago with Pupul Jayakar, the dynamic doyenne of Indian arts, confirmed my feelings. She referred to Central Asia as the source of power that created the succession of styles on the Indian subcontinent. "Go beyond the North West Frontiers," she said, "and discover there this wellspring in simple, hearty tribesmen."

An opportunity came to do this when I was invited by Queen Hope of Sikkim to visit her in late summer of 1972, a few weeks after I would be going to Istanbul for a World Crafts Congress. In between would be a good time for Afghanistan. Rereading Marco Polo and James Michener's *Caravans* began my research.

On a gray afternoon in January 1972, our German fabric printer, Horst Zimmer, drove me to the Frankfurt airport for the flight to Afghanistan, only to find the airline counter closed. Considerable inquiry and finally a call to Kabul revealed this was the season when all Afghan planes went to Mecca. I flew over Paris on a plane that would put down at Beirut, Baghdad, Tehran, Kabul, and Karachi. The front-cabin passengers were mostly well-dressed, dark-haired college students going home for the holiday. I amused myself guessing who would deplane where, but was often wrong.

The Afghan Collection, displayed here in our expanded New York showroom, combined prints and woven silk patterns drawn from Central Asian warp ikats. As shown, two related all-loop wool Wilton carpet patterns could be combined in a number of ways.

On my arrival in Kabul, the health officer gave me a series of exotic immunization shots, then told me to stay in bed for thirty-six hours. That, of course, was impossible. Having come to arrange a longer trip that summer, I was to leave for Bangkok in two days. I understood that two Land Rovers with drivers and a guide would be required so that, if one car broke down, the other could go for help. I reserved the cars for August and checked into the Intercontinental Hotel, on the site of an ancient palace overlooking the city. When I set out for the market a little later, my first surprise was seeing all the women veiled, and many of them totally covered by tentlike chadors with only small holes for eyes and mouth. The weather was cold, the countryside snow-covered, and the market stalls few. A nearby street of antiques vendors, however, was a bonanza. Fully stocked with incredible treasures, especially textiles, the dealers had not seen a buyer in weeks. As it was a weekend I couldn't wire for money, so I bought fabrics to the limit of my travelers' checks, including a magnificent felted camel blanket and Bukhara ikats that became the genesis of our Afghan Collection in 1974.

Hoping to obtain an invitation to visit the tent encampments of nomads in northern Afghanistan, we treated the children to hard candies. Some tribes refused entrance; others, warmly hospitable, fulfilled my desire to connect with the vitality of the Central Asians.

In August I returned to Kabul with my American friends the furniture maker Sam Maloof and his wife, Frieda, the jeweler Ramona Solberg, and the sculptor Risa Sussman. After a few days in the capital we flew to ancient Herat near the Iranian border, famous for its blue mosque. Near the mosque we came upon a nomadic tribe arrested for attempting to drive their fattened sheep into Iran. Through the gate of the walled city came three generations of men, women, and children; and horses, camels, sheep, and goats – two thousand animals in all. Our carriage horses reared up at the sight of this throng, not unlike the parade of captive Nubians in *Aida*! Then, it was back to Kabul, and off to Bāmiān and the north, in two four-wheel-drive Peugeots. The agent explained that because the desert we were to cross was held by pirates, we would travel only on roads, where the sedans would be more comfortable than Land Rovers.

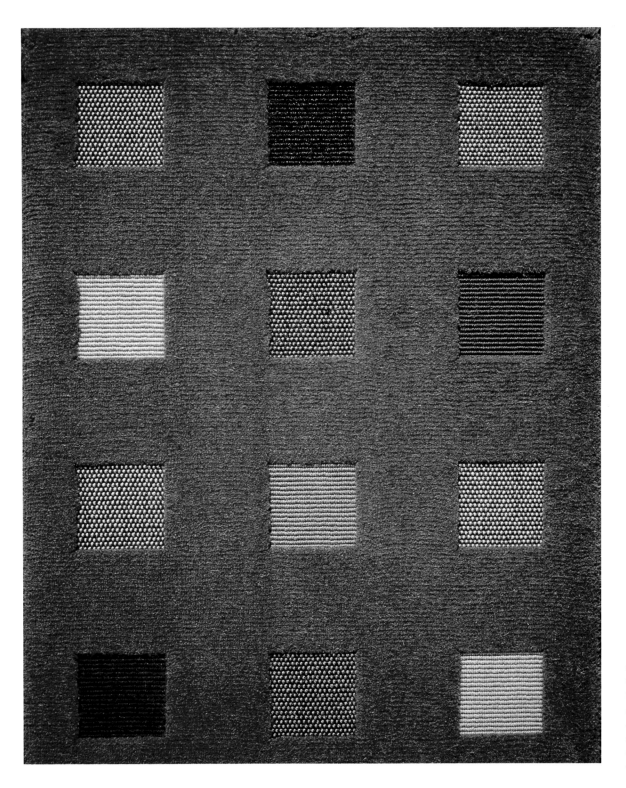

Inspiration for our Quadrangle carpet came from an ancient mosque in Afghanistan. The red sandstone, weathered to a soft matte surface, was studded with recessed glazed tiles that seemed clear and moist by comparison. For the carpet, I modulated squares of various colors of lustrous loop pile well below the dull cut-pile matrix.

Our party was delighted to find the American Embassy a comfortably informal clubhouse for activities including exhibits and films for English-speaking residents. After the spartan, Russian-built guesthouses in other cities, the relative luxury of the rooms and communications center at the Intercontinental were also welcome.

Bāmiān is best known for an ancient Buddhist monastery housed in caves carved out of a sheer cliff and later laid waste by Genghis Khan. Equally remarkable in this arid land was a broad valley, lush and green, with grain fields and a fine allée of poplars nearly a mile long. In spite of the cool night we slept comfortably in felt yurts and in the morning headed north. Risa, who arrived in Kabul early, had the chance to dine with a minister who invited us to the king's hunting lodge high in the mountains. His only request was that we bring sugar for the staff there. All day our cars climbed up a tortuous, boulder-strewn dry riverbed. When we arrived near dark, the staff at the lodge was alarmed to see motor cars; none had been there before, as the king and others came on horseback. If the modern lodge was more comfortable than palatial, the views across the azure and rose mountains at sunrise were unforgettable. Driving back down the river bottom was only a little easier than the ascent. When we reached the road, both drivers knelt on prayer mats. Their explanation was, "We thank Allah for Peugeot!"

Alexander the Great's old capital, Mazār-i-Sharīf, now almost on the Soviet border and tainted by Russian modernity, was disappointing, its ruins reduced to grassed-over mounds. The most powerful sights were ancient caravansaries. These caravan stopovers towered over the plains with fortified walls on a scale sufficient to protect many men, horses, and camels against armed attack.

Much more to our liking was Kundūz, the flower city in the northeast, where the population had swollen with Uzbek refugees coming south to escape the Soviet takeover of Uzbekistan in the early 1920s. As we drove into Kundūz I noted a street full of stalls. Soon there, I looked up into the narrowed eyes of an Asian rug dealer. "You are Uzbek!" I called. "Yah," he said, flashing gold teeth as he held out a hand to pull me up onto the floor of his wooden stall. Kyrgyzstani rugs on the walls were patchworks of heavy, brilliantly colored felt, up so long the nails were rusty. In minutes, all were mine! An assistant folded

them as the shopkeeper gathered neighbors in for a celebratory tea. That day and for the next two afternoons, six of us sat in the bare stall taking tea and fruit while engaged in a lively exchange more profound than language. Communicating through sign and body language or acting out, one of these Uzbek merchants described traveling with a caravan to Chinese Turkestan. Another had secretly ventured back to Bukhara to discover that his nomadic people had been forced to settle near new cotton mills. All were opposed to Russian militarism and curious about America. Our visits ended with much laughter, much tea, and small presents, as our cars were piled high with bags of fabrics and rugs for the return to Kabul. Although we visited some tented nomadic groups – one with a hospitable young mullah dressed in white robes and looking like Jesus Christ – none of the Afghan experiences was more rewarding than my brief meeting and hearty rapport with the Uzbek traders.

Afghanistan then, before the hippie and Soviet invasions, was a step back in time: the Bible could be filmed there without change of costume. Sun-bronzed, bearded men in turbans winnowed grains on the same threshing floors employed by the ancient Sumerians. Endless flocks of grazing animals included fat-tailed sheep weighted with bustles sufficiently large to sustain them for weeks without food or water. While some herders lived in the black felt tents of bedouins, round yurts with conical roofs were more common. In frail cloth tents as patched as a crazy quilt, other nomads and their foraging animals camped in farmers' fields. With farmland so precious and farm work so hard, we clearly understood continuing feuds between planters and herders.

For all its scenic beauty, with a hundred peaks as vertical as the Matterhorn, this is a harsh land in terms of life support. It is bitter in winter, scorched in summer, and arid in all seasons. Irrigation permits limited agriculture, the most notable crop being honey-sweet melons. Only through courage and persistence can these Caucasian and Asian peoples garner subsistence from an empty terrain. Knowing hardship so well, they are open, even generous, with strangers. Having risen for work before dawn, the men can be observed at day's end in teahouses – quiescent, stoic, philosophical, and seemingly oblivious of time.

The most lighthearted aspect of this dun-colored countryside was the painted Mercedes and Volvo open trucks. Usually painted on a ground of green, every surface was covered with blossom and tendril patterns as carefully composed as their silk-embroidered prayer shawls. As cars were few, these trucks dominated road traffic, carrying goods and livestock but mostly people. The jolliest were groups of dancing boys. With ironclad taboos on both female exposure and adultery, these lads were considered a barrel of fun.

The last phase in Kabul was packing up and shipping out. Wanting to make a sea shipment worthwhile, I bought many antique fabrics and seventeen kilims. First these had to be approved for export by the National Museum, then the shippers told me we would have to "airlift the lot to at least Beirut as the road through Pakistan is full of pirates." The heavy cases and a steep air bill were worth it. As many of the fabrics were Central Asian ikats, I learned new technology and, at first hand, new imagery. Particularly for our Afghan Collection, I used both. Our production ikats began to find a market; the ikat patterns, woven and printed, enjoyed a field day; and the seed for my book and exhibition *The Dyer's Art* was planted.

SIKKIM

My invitation to Sikkim, the small kingdom in the Himalayas, came from Hope Cooke, the American wife of its ruler, the chogyal. Following our tour of Afghanistan, Risa Sussman accompanied me down to Delhi, east to Calcutta, and then over Bangladesh to the Darjeeling airport. From there we motored to the royal guest house at the foot of the Himalayas. At 5 A.M. we began a tortuous, all-day ascent by jeep, up a rocky burro path dangerously washed out by the monsoon. Because the door was missing on my side of the jeep, I had to hold on with both hands to keep from falling into the winding river gorge below.

The hellish ride ended in the capital of Gangtok, a cool paradise filled with rhododendron trees. After weeks of camping in the desert, the small palace in an orchid garden, with the great snowcapped Annapurna looming over it, was a piece of heaven. A steward greeted us at the palace guesthouse, checking to see if our attire would be fitting for presentation to the chogyal. We arrived at the palace before dinner to exchange scarves, a formal rite to avert the need to prostrate ourselves in the royal presence. While we took champagne in the gardens, formally dressed ministers and their wives approached to a set distance, then fell straight – nose to the ground – until he bid them rise. This was repeated for the queen, after which everyone could behave naturally. We were grateful for our scarves.

During the daytime we visited the great Buddhist monasteries of this theocracy, the craftsmen with their fine metalwork, and the queen's small workshop for knotted Tibetan carpets. Rising early, I would walk into the town as the tradesmen opened for the day. Sacred cows, knowing which shops were Hindu, would stick their heads into doorways for morning handouts. One evening the chogyal spoke to us about India's stranglehold on his landlocked kingdom and of pressures from a native population administered by his Nepalese minority. Other than that, life was quite satisfactory. Sikkim was reputed to have the finest wine cellars in Asia. The few foreign diplomats in the small capital were happily living there as a reward for past services.

One day our steward announced that there would be dances after dinner, which we assumed would be ethnographic. Instead, we were taken to the ballroom of the first, still unfinished hotel, where a rock band was playing a benefit to buy an electric guitar! The sight of ministers boogying in floor-length Tibetan robes was unforgettable. We left Gangtok near the end of these tranquil times. When pressure mounted, Hope and her children moved to New York. The chogyal, ill during a local uprising, unadvisedly asked for aid from New Delhi. The Indian army simply annexed his kingdom, confining the chogyal to palace arrest.

CHINA

If my entrance into China and its silk industry came about slowly, it greatly enlivened our fabric design in the mid-seventies. My first invitation came through China's ambassador to Canada, who was, prior to the revival of U.S. relations with China, organizing exchange tours for ten North American architects and ten entrepreneurs; which group would I join? When I learned the latter group would include Marshall McLuhan, Stanley Marcus, and other interesting leaders, I decided to join them and to see the architecture along the way. Wrong! It didn't work out that way. The architects enjoyed a red-carpet tour through twenty-six cities; then Beijing decided the entrepreneurs were too allied with capitalism and canceled our trip. Instead, the fashion designer Bill Blass and I were each invited to survey the potential for China silks. When the Chinese felt insulted by Bill's baldly negative responses to questions like, "Wouldn't this be wonderful in New York?" my invitation was delayed until the first Canton Fair after President Nixon's famous visit in 1972. In my evaluations of the Chinese fabrics, I would suggest that they pin up all the alternatives.

Then I could say, "This cloth is more appropriate than the others because . . ." It worked! I was asked back four more times, first to Canton, then to Beijing and Manchuria, where our heavy tussah silks are produced.

Designing for Chinese production was difficult, partly because designers did not exist there, partly because almost all silk was woven in its natural state, without dyeing. On top of this was the enormity of the operation: China Textiles (ChinaTex) was a far-flung confederation of twenty million workers. We could not address an individual but only "the responsible people at ChinaTex"; if our telex came from Larsen New York, our man in China would usually respond. From the beginning, the answer to my request for active design specifications was, "When you are an *old* friend of China, we can cooperate together!" When the architect I. M. Pei asked us to help on his Fragrant Hill Hotel in Beijing, I felt designing fabrics to remain in China might give us a wedge. It did not; instead we were told to do whatever we wanted outside China so as not to complicate matters at ChinaTex.

From the first I had been taken with the timelessness of rural China, where the landscape and the field workers, in coolie hats and carrying two baskets balanced on a shoulder pole, are little changed from those in paintings a thousand years old. In cities I questioned the identity loss between men and women, and from one individual to another. And what took the place of the art that had been eliminated as a token of the ancient regime? The postage stamps were one of the few expressions of visual beauty. So were the fresh vegetables that poured into the cities each morning. I have never seen them so perfect. I had a feeling that all those who came to see were not just stocking their larders or greeting friends. Instead, there seemed to be a spirit of communion with a verdant rural tradition and with beauty itself.

Industrialization was remarkably uneven. An amusing invention was the powerloom-weaver's stool mounted on steel rails so that a seated weaver could zoom over to inspect a loom thirty feet away. Equally amazing were the miles of handmade lace curtains and blocks of hand-knotted red corridor carpets, both imitating the machine-made.

My visits to Dairen (also known as Ta-lien), the port city of Manchuria, were the most interesting. This was partly because I was totally removed from Westerners, partly because the culture was exotic even to Chinese. As this area is cold in winter, the buildings were of brick and stone, with steep tile roofs and many

chimneys. Rebuilt by the Japanese in the 1930s, Dairen looked rather like a Scottish town from the last century. A few exceptions were small villas much influenced by Frank Lloyd Wright. I was at first impressed by having been given the presidential suite with a fine balcony overlooking a large round park. The reason was that all our meetings took place in my suite. At dawn I would watch groups in the park wait for sufficient light to follow a leader in tai chi. In many groups, perhaps a thousand people would perform in unison the ancient martial art. Then they would leave, and another shift would form. Older women, no longer working and often with bound feet, would stand on the sidelines to go through the motions again.

Manchuria retains many carryovers from Japanese occupation. Most of China is so densely populated, with so few leisure areas, that one-seventh of the people have Mondays off, one seventh Tuesdays, and so on. Manchurians take off Sunday. When the weather permitted, my group left the city for a men's beach club. Like Japanese, they all bathed in seawater before swimming.

The China project was exciting and fun, except for the banquets. Whether I was the guest of honor or the host, I had to stay until the end and keep eating. The banquet at the Winter Palace was thirty-two courses and six hours long! What a treat it was when, after I came out of China, my friend Charlotte Horstman took me to Gaddi's in Hong Kong, the best French restaurant in Asia. Subsequent to that last trip we were able to effect our purchases through the Chinese Mission in New York.

INDIA

When Pupul Jayakar, the director of the Handloom Board, invited me to India in 1960 to work with her new Weavers' Service Centers, she asked, "Pierre Cardin is coming for fashion; will you explore the possibilities for interior furnishings?" I agreed to go if my associate Win Anderson could join me. But would we like it? Half of my well-traveled friends found this subcontinent the most engaging destination; others rushed, almost on arrival, for the first plane out.

To me, India was the most fabulous of nations – the ultimate destination. At ten, through reading the adventures of Richard Halliburton, I already knew the Indian subcontinent to be once the great heart of a pink swath of empire stretching around my globe, from Palestine on the Mediterranean to the

Malay Peninsula and Singapore. The British Raj itself extended from the Tigris to Mandalay, including countries we now know as Pakistan, Bangladesh, Burma, India, and Sri Lanka. Larger and more diversified than all of Europe, India had been the quest of Alexander the Great and Vasco da Gama, the subject of Kipling and Somerset Maugham.

In the old issues of *National Geographic* I had pored over in fourth grade, this country outstripped all others as the land made for adventure. Even the animals – working elephants and camels, tigers, and giant serpents – fascinated me. The exotic people we read about, maharajas and swamis, Gunga Din and Mahatma Gandhi, seemed larger than life. The small Indian collection at the Seattle Art Museum when I was a boy had vastly expanded in the lantern slides shown by Dr. Sherman Lee, then professor at the university.

Just when I was starting to weave I met Elizabeth Bayley Willis, who had recently returned from two years in India gathering textiles. She introduced me to color as I had never seen it. Earlier I had thought I was weaving Indian color in my simple cloths, but these were the heady hues of the just-published Ajanta cave paintings, with blues played against earthy oranges like reflections in copper. In the Willis saris was a whole new kind of color, incredible admixtures of yellow-greens and red-oranges, of plums and apricots. They reflected the colors of Indian miniatures and Mughal flower gardens, with white used as a color against piercing yellows and oranges exquisitely balanced by whole ranges of pinks and lavenders.

These fantasies were not dulled when I experienced the splendid Indian textiles Mrs. Jayakar had assembled for Edgar Kaufmann's Indian textile exhibit at the Museum of Modern Art. Installed so sensitively and sensually by Alexander Girard, they became my impossible dream.

Arriving in Bombay at 3 A.M., we caught a few hours' sleep and a bath to be ready to face up to our first grand buffet in the Taj Mahal Hotel dining room. The lavish spread was appropriate for Indians and guests preferring food that is vegetarian or not, sweet or hot, local or cosmopolitan. In private homes – often family complexes – the casual seating of a buffet meal also precludes the convention of seating by rank. At a Parsi dinner we attended, the mother was seated at the head, her several sons next to her, then the daughters, then the son's wives, then cousins. I was slotted in with the sons, Win with the wives. No wonder Indian girls look for Catholic husbands from Goa! The only other solace is in someday becoming the matriarch.

At this lunch we first experienced the sensuous pleasure of eating with the fingers of the right hand, often abetted by pieces of warm Indian breads. Afterward we moved on to the large, comfortable studios of the local Weavers' Service Center. Mrs. Jayakar explained to the designers assembled that our objectives were to merge creative design with the traditional skills of India. Could Win and I, with our understanding of the international market, connect India to a clientele beyond its borders? Here and in the other Weavers' Service Centers we visited, this proved a formidable challenge.

For the most part, neither designers nor weavers had ever seen draperies or upholstered furniture, but assumed such fabrics to be deficient in structure, too flimsy for cutting and sewing garments, and lacking durability. Texture (which they understood to be in vogue) was perceived as a surface unpleasant to the touch, usually woven of coarse jute. As the designers and weavers were of different castes, they couldn't really communicate. The designers seldom descended to the weavers' dim, low-ceilinged workplace. But to everyone's consternation, I did. As the name suggests, pit looms have a small pit for the weaver's feet to work the foot treadles. In a hot climate this is pleasantly cool, while the tamped earth floor on which he sits is convenient for spreading out bobbins. The swarthy weavers, usually men, were remarkably nimble, patient, humble, and wise. I gained great respect for these craftsmen and their wealth of skills.

Win and I searched for yarns, cloths, and patterning systems that might lend themselves to upholstery, drapery, and wall coverings. We sought specific avenues to translate Indian textile traditions for the Western market. Where and how could great craftsmanship from India enrich Western rooms? Could we provide agreeable work for weavers trained to meet the needs of a rapidly disappearing royal patronage?

Our work was interspersed with interesting diversions. One Sunday we visited the English photographer Stella Snead at her cottage on Juhu Beach. We were amazed to see groups of Indian men walking the shoreline in formal black suits complete with pointed black shoes. The women, often Stella's subjects, entered the gentle surf fully clothed in sodden saris.

Living at the Taj was a wonderful way to comprehend the fading glory of the British Raj. This magnificent monument to Anglo-Indian style, built in 1911 as the major focus of a gateway to India, was as grand and old-fashioned as when Kipling had

been a guest. Room boys slept in the vestibules of our rooms, presumably to protect us and to fetch tea when we awakened. The vast plaza in between the hotel and the circular bay had views stretching to the island of the legendary Elephanta shrine. Across the water was the gleaming sphere of a new atomic-energy station; around the triumphant arch commemorating British domination milled a colorful crowd, including sooth-sayers and snake charmers. This magical place evoked India's ancient past and recent upheavals, its great human drama and tantalizing future.

We then visited Ahmadabad, feeling more at home in this cotton-mill center near the Pakistan border. We were guests of the Sarabhai family, whom I had met through John Cage. They, with vision worthy of the Medici in Florence, established the Calico Museum of Textiles and the National Design Institute. They also patronized the ancient Kathakali dance company and traditional craftmakers such as the women who decorated house walls with clay and dung reliefs imbedded with mirrors. At the same time they brought to India such luminaries as Le Corbusier, Louis Kahn, and Charles Eames. Ahmadabad is also the home of the Gandhi Sabarmati Ashram, with its fine papermaking studio.

As artist-in-residence at Vepar Studios in Ahmadabad, India, I explored a dozen hand-craft traditions. This was mostly in textiles, but included others such as these small hand-hewn stone tables (right). Within the broad spectrum of fabric embellishment, I screenprinted special cloths from Calico Mills and explored traditional *bandani* tie-dyes (above), as well as all kinds of patchworks and appliqués.

At the Gandhi Museum there I had one of the most moving experiences of a lifetime. The museum itself was small and the spaces within it diminutive, because of both Gandhi's stature and his stressing the humanity of people instead of power and palaces. Architect Charles Correa further reduced scale by laying out the museum into a checkerboard of open courtyards and square galleries. Each of the ten galleries was divided by meter-high partitions to focus on viewing a year in Gandhi's life (in photographs and quotations) at a time. Finally there was Gandhi's death, his funeral pyre, and, in the last vignette, a photograph of the possessions he died with: a loincloth, sandals, eyeglasses, and a cotton spindle. Win and I both had been very taken with Correa and his beautiful wife, Monica, when we met them in Bombay.

When the Sarabhais gathered for a daily luncheon meeting, Win and I were assigned to a visitor's table in the canteen. The only other guests, the French photographer Henri Cartier-Bresson and his assistant, ignored us from the far end of the long table. One day we arrived with our last great selection of old painted and embroidered fabrics. Waiting for lunch, we spread out some of our new treasures. Cartier-Bresson suddenly came to life, asking where we had bought them. When we explained that the shops were now empty because of our extravagance, the photographer asked to buy one. We gave it to him to effect more cordial relations. A wiser person would have traded it for a choice of photographs!

In Delhi, the artists at our Service Center were both cosmopolitan and fun-loving. I celebrated Holi, the festival of spring, with them, which ended in a bacchanalian revel on a rooftop. During this festival of a few days in February or March, people buy brilliant powdered colors from street vendors to emblazon friends and white sacred cows, all to commemorate the Hindu god Lord Siva's marriage. The processions, dancers, and drum players who wind through the streets are riotous fun, but one should attend in washable clothes! In Delhi we also met three agreeable young women who worked on the design of India's World's Fair pavilions and trade shows. Their deep understanding of East and West was extremely helpful. With them we watched Kathakali dancers being transformed by costumes and greasepaint into fearsome demons. We explored Delhi's ancient temples, mosques, and bazaars.

Win and I were entertained at parties in Pupul Jayakar's palatial salons, which – devoid of furniture – resembled painting galleries. Walls were decorated with large Rajasthani hangings painted on cotton cloth in luminous colors. The air was scented by tree roses brought down from a roof garden, while the festive saris of the guests expressed the exuberance of ballroom scenes on the operatic stage. Better yet were lively conversations with Indians who had been in Paris or London the week before, who attended Parliament that day and read the latest publications. Here was an aristocratic and responsible elite, free from the constraints of earning wages and so able to embrace the broad interests we associate with the Age of Enlightenment.

While in Delhi we had time for theater, museums, and the dealers selling Indian miniatures. After a solid introduction to the best of these small paintings, our taste developed to the point that we could not afford those we most desired. Instead, we bought a dozen handsome books on Indian painting, printed locally at modest prices. The galleries of the Handcraft Board were also tempting, with outstanding examples of contemporary work in lacquer, bronze, alabaster, turned wood, and textiles. Crates full of purchases were all packed on the spot and shipped home.

The ancient city of Benares was startling for its narrow winding streets, faded facades bordering the Ganges, and the crowds of rich and poor coming to bathe in the sacred river. Many had come to die in this holy place. One day while coming back from enjoying dawn on the river, we saw familiar eyes behind a white-painted face above a tall body, naked except for a loincloth. The mysterious figure put a finger to his lips indicating silence, then glided off. It was Vadarajan, whom we knew in New York and London as a dapper chargé d'affaires, there to light his father's funeral pyre.

As Clark's Guesthouse was considerably outside the city, we had to make a daily commute through its ancient narrow streets. On the road in front of Clark's was an impressive lineup of transport including rickshas and bicycle rickshas, automobiles in all sizes and conditions, and, finally, a selection of small elephants. After our car stalled on the first day in lanes choked with pedestrians, I opted for a young elephant. He was a gorgeous fellow wearing a brass neck bell on a turquoise silken cord, with yellow, green, and purple flowers drawn in chalk on his ears and trunk. Riding him was a great solution, because pedestrians melted into doorways as we approached.

These Indian vendors hawk brilliant pigments during Holi, the annual color festival. Buyers rub the colors over white sacred cows and on their friends.

When Win's persistent cough deepened into double pneumonia, she was flown to a hospital in Delhi. I was taken to Madras, where one of my assignments was to find a market for the million yards of bleeding madras cottons stockpiled in warehouses. When this colorful handweave was popular abroad, village after village had taken up its production. But with the craze for madras finished and the Indians refusing to abandon their illusion that fashion was cyclical, like crop failures (assuming that next year the Americans would buy again), I had to explain that such fashion cycles could take ten, even twenty years to repeat. I directed them toward the production of table napkins, madras patchworks, and stencil printing over the familiar checks. All of these avenues worked to some extent.

From Madras, we drove south along a resplendent, palm-edged coastline. Beyond the palms the glittering Indian Ocean tempted us to swim, until the driver warned us of sea serpents. Past the charming former French colony of Pondicherry, we came to the ancient religious center of Kanchipuram. While the earliest shrines at Ajanta and Elephanta had been hewn out of caves, the oldest temples here were carved from huge, solid boulders. There were also colossal bas-reliefs and an entire shrine of stone cows, long since washing into the sea. Another temple held huge figures mounted on wooden wheels, to be pulled by hundreds of devotees during festivals.

One afternoon while resting near an elephant watering tank, we watched a young woman enter the water to bathe and simultaneously wash her saffron-colored sari. She carefully stretched it over the warm stone steps to dry, and, wrapping one end around her, lay down like a cocooned silk moth. When she and her sari were dry, she adroitly arranged its folds and walked away, as graceful and voluptuous as an ancient sculpture.

Through an introduction from Pupul Jayakar, I met the sari weavers of Kanchipuram, the visual highlight of our whole Indian sojourn. While sari cloth for the middle class was often in the deep shades of semiprecious stones, the Kanchipuram saris captured the brilliance of begonia blossoms. The vibrant pastels, weighted with heavy gold brocading, combined light and color as effectively as Indian miniatures.

At the Weavers' Service Center in Bangalore the focus was on slubby silks frequently woven in the shimmering checks and iridescent taffetas still popular for draperies. This charming small city had been an important "hill station" where both

Indians and Anglos retreated to escape the heat of summer. Known as the Flower City, in February it was already awash with perennial borders at once resembling English gardens and Mughal court paintings. This was my first experience with South Asia's early summer. April is sometimes the hottest month, but usually May has this honor. From then on the monsoon rains cool the air until early autumn. Consequently, by February, even in the north, Indian women switch from silk to crisp cotton saris. How I appreciated the many streets in Bangalore lined with mature shade trees! Even more, I empathized with the English who had retired here to garden year-round, with abundant sun and affordable staff.

Leaving India, we stopped in Bombay for debriefing and farewells. Lady Tata of the powerful Parsi family, which owns Air India (and so much else), insisted I motor out to her trade school for orphaned boys. In contrast to the poorest weavers, who never failed to offer us a stool to sit on and a glass of cool water, Lady Tata did neither. But she was the exception.

Indian women bathing in saffron-colored saris celebrate water for its cool renewing and cleansing properties.

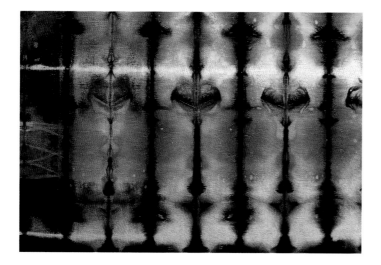

In the fold-dye resist patterning of Chan-Chan one perceives liquid dye migrating into a thirsty cotton cloth. Long bolts of this cloth were accordion pleated by fifty women standing in a line, then tightly bound with string, as revealed by cord marks on the selvage (left).

Throughout our eight-week sojourn, Win and I enjoyed the attentive consideration of all our requirements. India in the sixties may have lacked many things, but civilization was not one of them.

KENYA

Win rejoined me in Bombay for the trip to Kenya and Israel. As we put down in Aden, at the bottom of the Arabian Peninsula, it was announced that the ground crew was on strike, and our cargo space was full of fresh vegetables that must be unloaded before the plane could take off. The temperature was 120 degrees in the shade and much hotter on the tarmac. The longer we delayed, the more unbearable our cabin would get. When I volunteered to head up a work party, several Indians joined me in stripping off pants and shirts. From deep in the hold to the ground level, we relayed the heavy crates, then tried to dry off before dressing. This done and on our way again, I was satisfied to have done some physical work, with a measurable result.

Our friend Bob Peterson had introduced us to the extraordinary fold-dye fabrics made by Eliza Wilcox on the edge of Kenya's frontier. She had learned this ancient tie-and-dye technique in West Africa. Then, after Nigerian independence, she traveled with her Kenya-born husband thousands of miles across the Sudan to his family homestead at Gilgil. Not far from the game preserves and base of the Leakey family, Eliza set up shop. She pioneered the first fabrics made in East Africa, where people had jumped from wearing animal skins into imported cloths.

Communicating with Eliza by letter and telex, we had first sent production quantities of Swiss cotton printcloths by freighter to the steamy port of Mombasa. When these mildewed, we airlifted others to Nairobi, on the high plateau closer to Gilgil. This was our first opportunity to interact with the designs as they were being produced. In West Africa these fold-dyes are worked in two-yard lengths. Here, fifty women had been trained to stand in a line, folding – to a drum beat – wide cloth fifty yards long. This long accordion pleat was carefully wrapped according to a pattern designated on measuring sticks, then dyed in large vats, dried, retied, and dyed again. The resulting patterns not only had strong vertical emphasis desirable for furnishings, but also remain the best example of a perceivable marriage of liquid dyestuffs and a thirsty cloth.

In Gilgil we developed the colorings and new patterns for velvet. We also worked in the new weave shop where the silky, long staple wool of Kenya's Lincolnshire sheep was being hand-spun into yarn, then simply woven as luxury cloths. It amused us that these newly trained weavers were so enthusiastic that they came back to surreptitiously weave in off-hours. Bouncing along in a jeep, we followed hundreds of ostriches and thousands of zebras across the plain. Around them we found exotic wild flowers decorating a land as beautiful as an unspoiled California.

ISRAEL

Our plane out of Africa to Tel Aviv was an El-Al carrier from Johannesburg, totally full with an already exhausted crew. We could not fly over Arab lands, but circled them by flying over Russia and around Turkey to arrive twenty hours later. Arthur Goldreich picked us up and introduced us to his new wife and design partner, Tamar de Shalit. We stayed at their house in the Herzliyya, a suburb laid out by her father, a cofounder of Israel. We learned about Palestinian cuisine, crafts, and customs, as Goldreich had become an enthusiastic champion of these gentle people. We met talented Israeli artists and designers, heard sad stories of kibbutzim, and saw remarkable demonstrations of an agricultural revolution. Our first visit to Jerusalem was the glorious close of a long trip.

IRELAND

Other trips included fifteen visits to Ireland in the 1960s, when the Irish Export Board invited me over to develop interior furnishings fabrics. It was a wonderful premise. At that time, the country's most conspicuous export was educated young men migrating to Canada, New Zealand, and elsewhere because no jobs were available at home. Small, pollution-free mills in the countryside could provide work for people in the towns and villages. As furnishings evolve slowly and sell steadily throughout the year, they offer stability to an industry outside the fashion mainstream. Ireland grew good wools; fine linens were available from the north, and the men sent to obtain my consent were both winsome and persuasive. The design workshops and sales gallery at Kilkenny Castle were already open, with a number of Scandinavian product designers working there. The Irish saw my advantage as having a distribution network. As our company could buy what we designed, an important link was secured with only the cost of my travel expenses. That a government felt good design was key to a successful resolution was appealing indeed!

Round Tower, our jacquard-woven worsted damask made in County Navan, is shown here draped over a battlement at Kilkenny Castle.

The numerous wools in our Irish Collection were produced on several of my many trips to Ireland in the 1960s. In 1969 I was photographed conducting a "weave-a-thon" at the Kilkenny Design Workshops. On the loom is Carrickmacross.

Also appealing was the rich green countryside and its gentle people who spoke as readily and musically as bird song. Billeted for weeks at a time at the old Royal Hibernian Hotel, I enjoyed Dublin as a walkable small city, full of history and stately Georgian architecture. I fused all this with considerable reading of Ireland's history, her poets and playwrights. In the evenings a new circle of Dublin friends hastened my assimilation.

Soon we decided to focus our project on a small jacquard worsted mill, another small mill not limited to yarns made on premises and therefore quite versatile, plus a Donegal hand-weaving operation on the northwest coast. The immediate problem was yarns. In an effort to adjust to a post–central heating market for lightweight tweeds "soft enough for the ladies," local yarns were no longer appropriate for upholstery. Moreover, the newer sheep herds were crossbred to produce both wool and meat, but not the best wool. For months we worked out new and old yarn types. Then, for a whole summer in our New York studio, we perfected weave densities and scoured finishes appropriate to these yarns. I incorporated the saturated, masculine colors of Ireland in these cloths, extending them to include smooth heathered satins and vegetable-dyed screenprints on both the satin and the tweeds.

At the end there was a spectacular exhibition in Dublin at the ultramodern library building of Trinity College. Considerable press resulted, as did openings of our Irish Awakening Exhibition across America and Europe, with generous backing from Ireland's distillers. The collection was a resounding success – even though my attempt to popularize Irish whiskey was not!

TRAVEL TODAY

I don't recall a time when travel discussions didn't involve someone, somewhere reminding us how wonderful it was *before*. Today, with more of us traveling, this kind of conversation is even more prevalent, and I have not been above it. How easy it is to rattle on about Athens when it was village scale with almost no traffic and no pollution, and the only accommodations sufficient for a prewar grand tour! One could go on indefinitely, comparing once unspoiled destinations around the globe. Long ago I heard that Bali, after World War II, was "finished." It seemed quite wonderful to me as late as the 1960s. Although it has been totally overrun since 747s started coming in from Sydney, there are still enchanting enclaves of lively expatriate communities and remote areas seemingly untouched.

How much better it is to focus on improvements. It's true that Bangkok was quite magical in 1960 but, then again, think about the four-hour-late planes slowly winding their way around the world. Or the tin-roofed barracks that served as an airport then, without air-conditioning even on the most blistering days. Ultimately companions are more important than places. Both the people visited and our traveling companions can make the less-than-wonderful memorable.

Our enthusiasms and our disappointments are both better when shared, best when both parties can contribute, whether as comrades, or as mentor and protégé. A change of scenery sharpens our awareness and often reveals virtues in an entourage. Now, twenty years later, leaving Bangalore for Calicut – not in an ancient car down a torturous, winding road, but flying quickly and according to the schedule – I was pleasantly surprised with the marked improvement since my first visit. Crossing the tarmac to board, I noticed this was not the small plane I expected, but a new 737. Suddenly my mind came into sharper focus: How can I presume to feel paternal pride in India's move into modernity – as if ancient Mother India, thousands of years old, subcontinental, home to a billion people, was coming of age because I believed in these sometimes exasperating people, their virtues, and the mellowed beauty of their country? Am I to judge such a world?

On this most recent trip, too, I became more resigned to the coexistence of states above and below par. That is, there are sights and sensations more spectacular and more sumptuous than we experience at home. "Try to focus on these," I tell myself, "and not on the delays, not on those with their hands out. Remember the perfumes of the spice bazaar, remember the thousand oil lamps flickering at dinner last night, and don't be impatient with this momentary delay."

Repeated travels to the Third World make me more aware of sweeping changes engulfing whole regions, as inevitably as the tide. And this reminds me of the mile-wide, flat, bleak ocean beaches of the Olympic Peninsula I knew as a boy. There, families in sedans "from inland" drove over hard-packed sand of a retreating tide to picnic near the pounding surf. When the tide suddenly turned, coming rapidly back, they quickly packed up to evacuate, only to find spinning car wheels now embedded into sun-softened sand. Oh, what panic, digging out with cake plates, blankets laid down for traction, everyone in the vicinity called on to heave and push, all to no avail! The tide rolled on, lifting the car and rolling it over in the merciless surf . . . a nightmarish end to a long-anticipated outing.

Thus, South Asia has been caught up in the tide of the late twentieth century. As recently as 1959, when I first visited Asia, these lands were timeless agrarian communities with age-old values unconcerned with time or money. How it has changed, how rapidly it continues to change. The Asian sense of time, perhaps not. But there is certainly a focus on money – making money through development, off one's own community, and greed on all levels. It's not that all of the old values are gone, but certainly they are less apparent. Instead of the old charm there is the glare of white paint already blackening with mildew, unshielded fluorescent lights, and the blare of pop music. Look away, look away . . . get past the stumbling blocks to the virtues remaining.

I have long believed that Japan and the Indian subcontinent will be the last truly Asian countries: Japan because her industrious islanders can afford, if they choose, to maintain traditions while embracing modernity at its cutting edge; Pakistan and India will keep aspects of the past alive simply because the geographic areas and the expanding populations are too vast for rapid total change.

THE QUEST FOR IDENTITY   I don't remember a time when I wasn't

seeking identity through a sense of place. Having succeeded growing radishes

at three, I collected, at four, seedling maples for the first "Jack's Garden" (and,

at ten, took some satisfaction in the colossal crane required to remove these

fast-growing trees from what became a house site). Although my first personal

gardens were organized by boundaries and walkways, they were primarily

collections of wildings captured from field and forest, induced to grow in leaf

mold, and to bloom. When taken along on the Sunday drives common to

the Great Depression, I would ask to be left off in promising sites to forage

for "strubs," including miniature Johnny-jump-ups or mosses, giant trilliums,

and flowering currants.

CHAPTER 4

An aerial view of Round House, taken before the four-level tower was added. Walled gardens and outdoor living areas complete the Bantu inspiration of round structures forming a compound. Wisteria vines over the glass-roofed conservatory are effective in providing summer shade but winter sun.

By five, and kindergarten, I had already started fulfilling a lust to create places, as did my contractor father, out of any material available, and any support team coercible: usually Barbara, next door and a year older, and her little brother, Rodger – in rompers, silent so as not to be left out, and gullible. Dad had built us a playhouse complete with a porch and window boxes, a swing, and a teeter-totter – all of which were too prescribed to really be ours, as the encampments were. The first of these were tents made of coverlets. Another was only a cool space we cleared within a thicket of Scotch broom, sufficiently secret to defy parental detection. There were treehouses and caves, ones built of logs, wigwams of interlaced branches, tepees stretched over lodgepoles, log cabins, and a two-penny circus. That their making was the object explains the construction of so many.

Our alternative activities were the expeditions to "discover" Big Rock, Big Pond, Lake Washington – not along roads, if there were any, but over land, through swamps and stingray nettles, with briars bloodying our clothes and tearing our stockings. Rodger would cry, Barbara would mutiny. For me, such adversities while wandering off into the unknown only brightened our final achievements. And perhaps, more importantly, the quest was to dream up projects for someone else to follow.

The summer I turned six we moved to Bremerton, the naval suburb across Puget Sound. Nearby neighbors, including Doris and Phil Meyer and their son George, would become my lifelong friends. George and a few other boys my age allowed for group expeditions and, particularly, the outfitting for them: towels if we found water for swimming, bent hooks for fishing, and provisions. As Phil Meyer owned a grocery, we hoped George would contribute rare treats. He always volunteered first, "I'll bring the water."

My family always lived on the edge of town. In Seattle, where I spent my first six years, this was on new streets near the University District. Close by were a stream draining farmed acres and the remains of an orchard. When I was two, the move to Northeast 20th Street put us on the edge of meadows and woods, with truck farms just beyond. In the spring, Italian women came to our meadow to cut dandelion greens and, at summer's end, Japanese families came for mushrooms. In winter, this same grassy hill, far from traffic, was just fine for sledding.

In Bremerton, we lived on or near Phinney Bay, with woods all around. Even when we moved during my high-school years to Capitol Hill, there was a square mile of nature preserve just two blocks away. In new houses with new gardens (like ours) there was some pleasure in planting from scratch, but I envied classmates who could bring armloads of magnolia branches to school.

As a young man I also moved frequently. Particularly in New York, there were few years without a move. Either I upgraded apartments, the showroom, or the design studio, or I expanded a warehouse. Although I became increasingly adept in space planning as we built showrooms in America and Europe, I never quite learned how long each build-out would take, nor the unforeseen expenses.

When I moved to New York, a sense of space became important. Partly because furniture was scant and low to the floor, my first studio/apartment in Arundell Clarke's townhouse had a flow of open space. Clarke loaned me a splendid custom-designed bed. From my new friend John Cage I learned of a mattress maker who would do custom sizes covered in my fabric. Two of these, boxed in a wood frame on either side of the fireplace, looked like garden beds until I raised them on legs cut from turned balusters. I was pleased when a comfortable chair in my fabric came from an exhibition in time for Barbara Dorn's visit. She brought the Danish furniture designer Jens Risom, who was so appalled by my empty spaces that he invited me to his showroom to select some furniture. Instead, I bought two lightly scaled campaign chairs and found great tabletops, one sufficiently large for Japanese dining. The plants I brought in from a country weekend luxuriated under a skylight. Before I moved out, *Vogue* photographed the white serenity of this top-floor oasis.

When the studio expanded to lofts on 22nd Street, I was too preoccupied with our growth to really move into my new apartment. Instead, we built out our first showroom at Park Avenue and 58th Street. For our company to afford this, I paid rent on the back room to use as my office and, with the narrow daybeds I had constructed, a bedroom at night. By comparison, my parlor-floor apartment on West 9th Street off Fifth Avenue was palatial. With fourteen-foot ceilings in the former ballroom and a baronial paneled library overlooking a garden, I did not complain about the makeshift kitchen and closets. A friend in Charleston found a pair of 1815 caned recamiers, which felt right in the space. I brought a huge kilim from Athens and

Every year at my Gramercy Park apartment I redesigned the interior as a means of experimenting with the cloths we were developing. The chief fabrics here, including those on the walls and ceiling, all stretch. Pierre Paulin's sculptural seating is covered with a printed warp-knit and a snug stretch wool we wove in Norway. Fabric panels on either side of the fireplace were printed with phosphorescent pigment to glow in the dark. Windows offered a choice of three different roller shades.

I was trained in interior architecture but seldom practiced except on my own digs. This cover story for *House & Garden* was sponsored by a Venetian-blind fabricator newly capable of laminating fabric to the blind slats. I added to the wall hinged shutters covered with two of our prints. When shutters were closed the room was quite transformed.

sufficient furniture to host my first New York parties at home. *Vogue* photographed this apartment as well, just before my move in 1960 to "Block Beautiful" – East 19th Street near Gramercy Park.

In that apartment Hans Knoll and Eszter Haraszty had stripped off moldings and opened up spaces. I had six rooms and two baths just a stone's throw from Larsen Design Studio. Working mornings with a secretary at home and afternoons and evenings in the studio became even better when the roof garden was equipped with a telephone and pergola to be an office in a flowery setting. Here I learned that building out evolving interiors was easier than moving: at least the book storage, closets, and kitchen were constant. At one point I centered a large, round, white marble table in the twenty-foot-square dining room and surrounded it with an enclosure of six-inch-wide antique gold ribbons, suspended on a circular track. From walls vertically paneled in natural maple flooring I hung a long credenza with a drop-down front for my secretary's desk. I worked on the dining table until coming home to a stack of homework became so intimidating that I converted a sitting room into a dark bedroom with a sunny, plant-filled office just beyond it.

As a setting for our Great Colors of China Collection, I finally built out the living room so bizarrely as to suggest it was time to move. The rented apartment at the Kips Bay complex was a convenient interim step. Although the ceilings were only the standard eight feet high, I. M. Pei's perfect proportions helped. One of the bedrooms had been added to the living room to create a thirty-by-thirty-foot window-walled space. I mirrored the ceiling in the remaining bedroom, then fitted it with banquettes covered with silks from our Afghan Collection. Compared to the airy naturalness of the large room, this one was from Arabian Nights.

When in 1980 my associate Win Anderson said it was time I had a townhouse, I found a spectacular loft. With vaulted ceilings, skylights, and a terrace, it was just a block from our Greenwich Village studio. My bid on it was turned down just as I was leaving for Beijing. When I described it to my friend Philip Cutler at breakfast the first morning there, he said, "Jack, this sounds so right for you; why don't you use my telex to up your bid?" The answer came back from my accountant, Will Diller, "You went up a bit more, but it's yours."

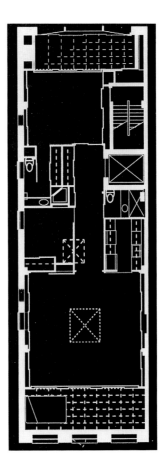

The advantage of loft living space is having no walls or fixed elements, so one can outfit it as freely as an empty birdhouse. Some lofts are also vast; this one on 10th Street was small but – with windows on three sides plus skylights, splendid barrel vaults, a terrace, and a location only a block from my studio – optimum!

Daylit and low-key, architectonic, rich in materials, and custom-built within an existing space, the 10th Street loft was as pleasant to be in alone as with a party. By using fabric-covered sliding panels on all the long walls, I could at once be rid of obtrusive pilasters and either conceal or reveal hundreds of objects and thousands of books. The floor plan indicates how compactly the space was organized.

Although uncluttered, the loft was not without sybaritic comforts. On the south ledge next to the terrace were a black soaking tub doubling as a reflecting pool, a bed covered in quilted silk, and a custom-built fireplace.

Next week, as I sat on the floor and worked on a low table at the Tarawaya Ryokan in Kyoto, trying to resolve the space plan of the loft, its spirit became increasingly Japanese. Fusuma sliding panels over the long walls would hide odd-sized pilasters and provide a hundred shelves for objects and books. At either end of the loft, where windows were a disproportionate thirty inches above the floor, I created raised platforms seven feet deep. Translucent shoji panels could close off front or back living rooms from the long entrance gallery. I decided to use Japanese plaster colored with clay and bound with broken rice straw. One could dine or sleep any number of places without specific dining rooms or bedrooms.

For a late-evening buffet supper the south room is all aglow. The daybeds have been stowed under the deck and storage boxes with seat pads rolled out along the right wall. The trestle tables came out of storage. Guests gathered for cocktails in the north room and then were led into this space.

On my return I handed my plan over to architect Charles Forberg, then left for Europe. Then I telexed him, "Above all, there is to be a sense of structure and materials not afforded in Park Avenue apartments." His masterful scheme created an exposed wooden space frame within the loft. Seven-foot-high, four-by-eight-inch fascias around all the rooms unified the space and concealed the tracks for suspending fifty-two sliding doors. Eight-inch floor tiles, glazed the color of milk, doubled the light.

When I called Japan House to ask if they knew of a Japanese contractor, they said they liked the man who built their place. With thirteen Japanese craftsmen Sam Takiuchi worked on the loft for a year. He added Portland cement to the Japanese plaster to accommodate changes in humidity. From Seattle, he obtained straight-grained fir cut from the huge virgin timber logs normally shipped to Japan. To keep the color of this wood light and cool, we painted the finished structure with slaked lime, then – wearing masks – rubbed off the lime with terry toweling. Flexible, with light from windows on three sides plus two skylights, easily accommodating a crowd but a delight to be in alone, this was the most perfect of the spaces I have lived in. Curator Stewart Johnson once said the whole of it should be in the Metropolitan Museum.

ROUND HOUSE

Most of the good things in my life have grown out of affairs of the heart. Becoming a weaver started out like taking a casual stroll on a hillside and falling into a pit from which I never wanted to climb out. My moves to Los Angeles and New York City were not so much decisions as giving in to the irresistible pull of a strong magnet. Certainly I didn't know that New York, as the design marketing and publications center, was the only logical base for a fabric designer. I came because of its cosmopolitan verve. Likewise, my trip to Africa was to fulfill a childhood dream of experiencing Bantu architecture.

As people did not go to West Africa in 1960, there was great curiosity about the Dark Continent. On our return, the press asked for so many interviews that our new public relations consultant said she would leave us if I did not design what would become our most successful introduction, the African Collection. This group of fabrics catapulted our small firm from being an insider's source to being as close as we would ever be to a household word.

Although now almost obliterated by weathering, the painted stucco walls at Round House added interest when plantings were young and small.

Nearby but private, the guest quarters at Round House were approached through a shady woodland garden often fragrant with orange blossoms, wild azaleas, lush ferns, or lily of the valley. When blooming in May, the maturing Asian cherry (left) becomes a great pink cloud attracting thousands of bees. These, in turn, are a magnet for orange and black orioles – smashing against the pale pink.

When Betty Pepis wrote about the round house models I had begun in Africa as if they were already built, many magazines, including *Life* and *Look*, asked to photograph them. This encouraged me to move faster, as it seemed that manufacturers might help me with building materials. That year I rented a chauffeur's apartment on Lily Pond Lane in East Hampton and then two bicycles to explore possible building sites. The built-up areas near the ocean appealed to me because of their ordered, timeless grace. Then I was shown fourteen acres on the edge of the Great North Woods. I could buy ten acres affordably, with an option on the other four.

As farmland worked until early in the century, the grassy meadows were pleasantly contoured and surrounded by a hedgerow of tall oaks, creating a picture-perfect private kingdom. Best of all were the sculptural cedar trees *(Juniperus virginiana)* parading into the distance like a Greek chorus. At the north end, an opening in a fine stand of well-spaced pitch pines determined the house site, which Win and I staked out with rope as a compass, then mocked up with three circles of snow fencing. Not far from this site were four old, dwarfed pines that would soon be on an island in the center of a lotus pond.

The house was intended as a simple shelter from the elements for those hours when my friends and I could not be out-of-doors (see page 94). Walled spaces between the round house, guesthouse, and studio would become outdoor rooms, creating a more intriguing composition than those of most small houses. I talked to several architects, but was most taken with Robert Rosenberg when he humbly asked to collaborate with me on the project.

Plantings would be contained within round, stuccoed walls to separate the ordered from the God-given. I had not intended to cut the meadow grasses either, but their summer height blocked our view of the new pond. These grasses were scythed until I asked my friend and adviser, landscape architect Robert Zion, how to determine the edges of planting beds. "Using a tractor mower," he answered, "will quite naturally make a graceful curve easy to follow for years to come."

Although the stuccoed houses could have been wood-framed, I felt they should be of masonry, like the African originals. They could have been concrete block but the builder, a carpenter, wanted to build wooden forms for poured concrete. All winter his team built forms, each weekend telling me the

Clockwise, from top:
When the original galley-like kitchen at Round House was opened up to a dining table in the living room, a curved door lowered to close it. The stoneware canisters were commissioned from Karen Karnes and Byron Temple.

Originally a round dining table was between the kitchen pass-through and the fireplace at Round House. Then it was in the conservatory. When the tower was added, its ground level became this large dining room, with a serving counter on the right, a tall fireplace, windows overlooking the plaza, and a hardwood ibis from West Africa.

The new dining room at Round House was on axis with a water work originating as a moat around Bill Moss's silver pavilion and finally cascading into the sunken garden. Studded with rows of pollarded sycamores, the plaza on either side provided firm footing for parties of up to two hundred.

The library/bedroom in the tower at Round House became a place for after-dinner coffee when the large bed folded into the wall. The broad window seat, with its padded backrests, was a fine place for reading with a view over the plaza. The stairs on the right lead to a fourth-level terrace.

The round living room was by day an airy pavilion with three tall doorways to the plant-filled conservatory. With the curtains drawn and a fire blazing it became a cozy refuge on winter evenings.

Below, left and right: Two views of the sunken garden reveal a stairstep cascade. From the terrace above, water alternates with beds flowering much of the year. The weave studio gains splendid light in what would otherwise be a dark basement.

Above: Walls and ceilings of the round silk room are shirred with pale tussah silk; the floor is unglazed terra cotta. All furniture, upholstery silks, and antique sculpture are from Thailand.

pouring would take only hours. It took days, but only after two more months of six men interlacing steel between the forms: the building code for poured concrete turned out to be a commercial one, appropriate for twenty-story buildings! In Africa building several round houses is economical, but not on Long Island. When I felt I could not afford to go forward with the studio, my builder suggested that we make it of the curved wooden forms of the living room. It did go up quickly, with little cost. The round, deep swimming pool was poured with the guesthouse forms.

My other intention was, as much as possible, to use crafts-men for site-specific commissions. This worked wonderfully! The principal players were potter Karen Karnes, who built two flameware fireplaces, the glazed stoneware plumbing fixtures, the switch plates, and the terrace furniture. She also created and fired – in a brickyard – the three four-foot rings surrounding the skylights at the peaks of the conical roofs. Erick Erickson cut and leaded stained-glass panels for the clerestory windows of four rooms and etched a bronze plate to screen the living-room skylight. I was buying directly at the maker's cost, with the pro-viso that if they were not given on-page credits when the house was published, I would pay double. These artists read architec-tural plans correctly and were among the few suppliers deliver-ing on time. Other craftsmen resolved production of my copper doors and incised stucco walls.

"WHAT IS ART?"
[A question to Pablo Picasso]

WHAT IS *NOT*?"
– Picasso

ON GARDENING
On occasion, when I ask myself why so much time and money go into my gardens, I know the reason lies deeper than my glib explanations to visitors. True, gardening is my favorite exercise and produces a satisfying bone-weariness at day's end. The satis-faction of gauging a day's progress by a new brush heap is real (even if less real than a new clearing or planting). It consoles me that the older gardener has superior wisdom, and (unlike tennis players) improves his game in the golden years – stiff joints notwithstanding! My identification with older, fully mature plant specimens as being the most prized is also alluring.

Gardening appeals to us all the more when we are caught up in the whirlwind beyond ourselves, in the great, natural life cycle. There dwells an underlying faith, a certainty that this sea-son's planting, pruning, and nourishing will be rewarded. Humility flourishes here as well; even master gardeners are but handmaidens to a superior life force only partially perceived.

There are, it seems, many different time cycles for planting. While arranging blooming plants permits immediate gratifica-tion, setting out small trees and shrubs – some destined to grow a hundredfold – requires extended vision. We take into account the plot plan, but must visualize the effect as seen in the full round. We go beyond the close-up to view the plantings at some distance. And then, imagine the next season: what follows the bloom and browning foliage? Ferns and virulent daylilies will mask yellowing daffodil foliage, or clouds of baby's breath will screen withering iris, but what happens after that?

I believe that most of us are tempted to compose young shrubs and trees according to their present size, just as we would arrange a still life, a table, or a bouquet. Reason then nudges us to double the spaces in between to allow for growth. This may be sufficient for some perennials but not for azaleas and young trees. It takes a leap of faith to imagine that young saplings may have a mature spread of sixty feet! When Round House was new I planted twelve-inch spruces, well separated, at the far edge of a meadow. At midsummer they were dwarfed by grasses and wildflowers, but, fifteen years later when twenty feet tall, only heavy equipment could lift every other spruce to create the space appropriate for mature trees. Now ten years older, they have again doubled their size.

One way to combat the compulsion to achieve composition from the first year is using surrogates to temporarily fill the empty spaces. Ground covers are a better bridge than mulch; annuals can also be employed. These spaces may be used for try-ing out various plants or as a nursery for baby trees. Even better are tall clumps of ornamental grasses to provide immediate height and bulk. When no longer needed as space fillers, they can be moved out more easily than woody plants. Traditional advice for planting street trees or an allée is to alternate the per-manent trees with fast-growing, inexpensive ones that can later be cut out.

Within a circular yew hedge adjoining the round walled pool is the blue garden at Round House. Bluestone pavers separate two-by-four-foot segments of either turf or flower beds to create a weave pattern.

As a designer, I find the garden a great teacher. "What is the lesson?" I always ask. "Why is a particular effect so pleasing or unsatisfactory?" In a dune garden or along the beach, I enjoy the nuance of highlight and shadow on gray foliage, or the shadow of wiry grass stalks bending with the wind to trace concentric circles on the sand. Why are these visual effects extraordinary? Because there are no distracting colors or dominating forms, no larger or darker shadows from overhead trees, no man-made intrusions to obscure their subtlety. This quiet beauty would not be noticed at the edge of an exuberant flower border; there, instead, the grasses would seem to be just waiting to be pulled out or whacked off. The lesson is clear: just as a great actress doesn't throw away her lines when drums are rolling, if a place is designated for such ethereal reticence, clear the stage for it.

For learning color, the garden is a master instructor, and not only during the brilliance of high season. Why is one of my favorite colorings that of dried bracken ferns in the winter sun, with their play of "moist" ribs against "dry" frond tissue? Because this color is low-key, I am more aware of the varied surfaces and underlying shadows. In the low light of winter the rusty gray of the fronds seems brighter against the subtle orange of the stalks

The first of Bill Moss's poleless silver pavilions for Round House hovered on the edge of the pond until a hurricane lifted it to destruction. Its successor became a dining pavilion within the bubbling water work on the new plaza. Moonbeams, our silvered solar cloth, reflected candlelight back into the magical space within.

and ribs. Dried gray lichens evoke a similar color play, but of bluish tones against yellow-green hues smoldering under hazy surface fibers. When I have attempted to replicate these low-key confections in textile surfaces, the elusiveness of success only heightens my awe of nature as designer.

Exfoliating barks are often beautiful in color as well as texture. The mottled olive greens of peeling sycamores and eucalyptus trunks are breathtaking orchestrations within a limited range of hue, chroma, and value. Western madronas and greasewoods roll thin layers of peeling bark into cylinders to reveal a dramatic play of red-greens and lacquer reds, all intensified by their own leafy backdrop.

Paper birch trunks, almost without color, startle us with their sharp contrast of dark branch wounds played against combinations of gray-white, chalk, and the translucent, fleshy tint of new bark layers underneath. The Siberian birch, *Betula sinensis*, is not only stately and resistant to leaf miners but also enchanting, as its whiter, pinkish underbark never loses a glorious youthfulness. Clumps of river birch, with peeling bark rolls as large as cigars, produce the most texture of all, in rosy tones of silvered cinnamon. Their coppery color is heightened when the trunks are revealed at eye level against a green winter lawn.

These reticent color combinations are a part of nature's palette, which I so much admire. Not that I don't enjoy the brilliance of sun-streaked cardinal flowers or ranges of blue iris against their silver-green foliage, or white-gold blossoms – like the trills of a piccolo – lighting up somber spring shrubbery. The sparkling white of trumpet lilies is perhaps my favorite "bright," but what can be learned from nature's exuberance, never ignoble even when combining vibrating corals with cerise? Purple orchids, perhaps vulgar as a corsage or table decoration, are breathtaking when blooming high up in trees shaded by overhead foliage, with the rainy season's verdure all around. If the strident annuals tarted up by hybridizers embarrass our suburban gardens, their natural counterparts look much at home with the effulgent companions of their habitat.

Most garden writers advise interplanting perennials with blossoms in contrasting colors so as to heighten their brilliance, but I am constantly playing down strong contrasts to focus interest on the whole. When Vita Sackville-West so successfully compartmentalized Sissinghurst by color, her purpose was to show contrast, not from plant to plant, but on the larger scale of room to room. Her walled-in cottage garden is such a ghetto for all the hot reds and oranges that would disturb other areas!

My favorite part of Sissinghurst – after the high walls of palest pink roses against ancient, orangy brick – is the somber forecourt with low, mounded forms so quiescent in color, so masterful in form as to be a moody prologue to the drama beyond. Here are all the mauves and lilac shades, which are often difficult, whether alone or in combination. Played against a full complement of blued and mossy greens, they make a contemplative statement, sufficiently grayed to blend with the court's stone pavers. In this way the whole space, not just the surrounding border, becomes an entity. If this were music, it would be a composition by Sibelius.

At LongHouse the purple garden has some of these same qualities, but with more sun and a palette widening from warm blues to the deep purple-reds of barberry and Japanese maples. Soft whites and silvery greens balance the yellow-green of grass paths. The play between the violet flowers and purple foliage brings out other greens, particularly the whited blue-greens of iris leaves.

It puzzles me that Western garden writers and others have an obsession with blossom color, when most of what we experience is foliage. The Japanese, on the other hand, are primarily concerned with form and texture through the seasons. To them rocks and water are paramount, as are carefully pruned pines with horizontal branches relating to the earth. While blossoms are exalted as they fleetingly appear, no flower is as keenly awaited as maple leaves turning color in November. My quest as well is for this kind of harmonious year-round orchestration. Life is too short to discard the months without summer bloom, or to look out only on winter-flattened perennial beds. I enjoy viewing the "bones" of the garden that are revealed after leaves have fallen. Then the hedges, walls, waterways, walks, and terraces come into their own, along with banks of conifers and broadleaf evergreens. Soon tall stands of golden grasses and still-green bamboos will be ornamented with hoarfrost, snow, or sparkling icicles.

We are perhaps too conditioned by two-dimensional painting and photography to easily comprehend the sculptural properties of gardens. When Isamu Noguchi was designing small parks, he would come to Round House to go through my tree books after the scheme was set, the lines of vision and the heights determined. He already knew where he wanted tall

At LongHouse, the first of a million daffodil blossoms show color in April. Come summer, this bed will be a sea of lady ferns dotted with spires of foxglove. Beyond it looms the house, with its bridge to the large berm parallel to it.

shadows on flat areas, where the visual incidents should be, where to contrast walls with water and shaggy textures. Only then did he determine which trees and shrubs would be appropriate. I, too, have learned to work this way on the larger aspects, but am more pragmatic in using what is on hand, what is a gift, or what I can afford to purchase.

THE LONGHOUSE PROPERTY

When I bought the first twelve acres at LongHouse, it was for protection along the north drive of Round House. I would have purchased a smaller strip, but my neighbor wouldn't sell less than the full width of his woodland. Instead, he offered affordable terms. By that time I knew the locale and what would thrive or balk in the dry, sandy soil.

The LongHouse acres had few of the amenities of Round House. Abandoned as farmland fifty years earlier, it was a vine-infested woodland of white and red oaks with a few pignut hickories. The land was flatter, with no protective ring of border trees. The pioneering cedars were long dead from lack of sun and the surviving pines had bare trunks from their tall heads down. The poison ivy, wild grape, and bittersweet vines scrambling up the trees were as thick as my arm. What were the assets, if any? A few beech groves, several native dogwood stands, and some ancient oaks. As ground covers, low bush blueberries flourished on some two acres, and a large patch of native ginseng spread over a shadier area. Everywhere several inches of leaf mold covered the sandy soil. The most interesting features were the long, low, straight-as-an-arrow berms that had been piled up as field borders when the land was farmed.

After clearing out fallen trees, vines, and saplings, I hired a backhoe to create wide woodland paths and two grassy meadows. The long berms were then planted with thousands of Canadian hemlocks, which were mail-ordered – bare-root and at most eighteen inches high. They had the advantages of tolerating deep shade and being affordable. Also bare-root and cheap, hundreds of small dogwoods, beeches, winterberries, and birches came into my nursery. Against drought, I ran a line of hose bibs a third of a mile long. There was no remedy for two successive years of gypsy moths; saving most of the baby beeches was all I could do. Progress was slow because maintaining the ten acres at Round House took most of our time. I learned to love the winters, when weekends could be devoted to clearing the new

LongHouse from the air reveals the main buildings aligned with long hemlock hedges and overlooking Peter's Pond, with the base of Roy Staab's bamboo sculpture floating in its center. The greenery of the Western Gardens at the top contrasts with the dry Dune Garden, appearing at the lower right. This ends at the Gate House and the shady Secret Garden above it.

Illustrated plan
of the LongHouse
property.

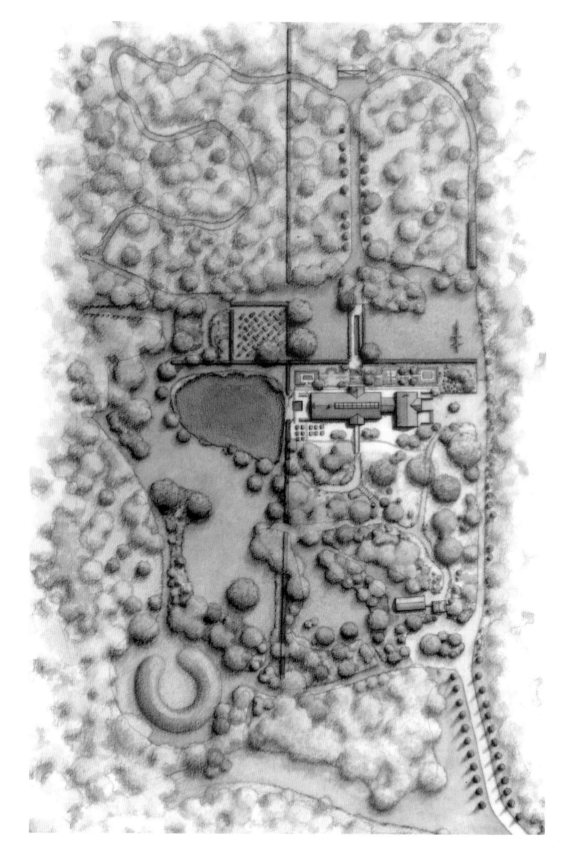

land in bold strokes. Then, when professional woodcutters could
bring in trucks to take out the logs, large areas were opened up
quickly. With burning no longer permitted we made frequent
trips to the brush dump with my new Ford pickup pulling an
enormous old trailer.

I was attempting to create large and small sun-filled spaces
within the woods and to induce evergreen walls to grow
between them. More paths were created. Bamboo from Round
House was moved along the other two berms; the first cryptomeria and western cedars were planted to establish winter
greenery and begin a surround for the Secret Garden. When a
long massing of Pfitzer junipers became too large at Round
House, they were pruned and transplanted to LongHouse for
another segment of this surround. Native mountain laurels were
collected from new housing sites. This was the start of a new
park, readied for the picnics and barbecues around my fiftieth
birthday.

I had hoped to build a large pond in an area about five
feet lower than the rest of the property. When a conservancy
team calculated that even with a pond liner there would not be
sufficient runoff, I wondered what else could be made of this
natural bowl. An earthwork? From building ponds I had learned
that the only aspect of gardening that goes quickly is moving
earth with a bulldozer. All this was resolved when I decided to
create a basement and sunken garden for the new tower at
Round House. We simply carted the subsoil over to the new
property. Remembering the ancient ring forts of Ireland, I
determined that we could build up a high, grassy ring that would
also serve as an amphitheater. Moreover, the lower side of the
bowl could also have an outer ring to baffle both the view and
sound of the road beyond. The earth was heaped in a circle,
then – before seeding – laboriously shaped to maintain a consistent radius, height, and pitch. Late in the autumn I added thousands of crocuses and snowdrops to the bowl, hoping to replicate
the momentary spring millefleur at Hidcote. This grand effect
materialized only the first spring; after that the voles found irresistible such a concentration of foodstuffs.

Standing in the bowl without being able to see anything
but a great cup of green grass, one felt detached from the rest of
the world. As acoustical properties were excellent, I hosted the
first concert there with the artist Larry Rivers's cool jazz combo.
Guests coming over from Round House were guided by tree
trunks banded with our brilliant Thai silks. Since then, the
amphitheater has been the setting for readings, dance perfor-

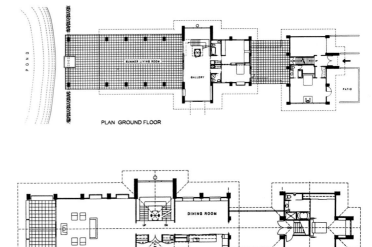

Plans of the principal
floors at LongHouse.
On the top level (not
shown) are a library,
home office, and writ-
ing studio. Below grade
are a small auditorium,
billiard and loom
rooms, and art storage.

Viewed from the luncheon table on the berm, the great roofs of LongHouse shade its walls and windows. In contrast, the bridge leading to the conservatory is so open to the sky and stars that it serves as a moongazing platform.

Opposite: As seen through the conservatory doors, the bridge serves as an easy transition from the second floor to the garden.

mances, and installations of sculpture. Most of the time it is simply a place of great quiet. The overhanging oaks have spread their branches low, softening the bowl's edges and expanding it upward. Soon creeping zoysia grass will cover the whole of it, eliminating the need to mow, weed, and water.

BUILDING LONGHOUSE

During the summer of 1986 in Santa Fe I again visited the sprawling adobe home of Linda and Stanley Marcus. More than the panoramic views over miles of untouched terrain, I was impressed by the generous flow of interior space. My own floor plans had always avoided such "waste space." Up alone at dawn, I enjoyed these spaces for exhibiting art and stretching the soul. I also became aware of how hospitable this house became when afternoon rains drove party guests indoors. Round House, even

LongHouse was just finished in this view across Peter's Pond toward the house and its imposing South Gate. The rafters crossing above the gable evoke the Ise Shrine, the seventh-century Shinto building complex that inspired the overhanging gabled roof and the raising of the principal rooms to the second level in order to gain vistas.

Three stories high, the stair hall is protected against western sun by the broad blades of jalousie shutters. The 380 elements of Dale Chihuly's chartreuse chandelier were blown in Seattle especially for this space. In daylight the glass appears to be in concert with the landscape and beyond. Here, at dusk, it is bathed with small floodlights.

The wide blades of whitewashed jalousie blinds dramatize the play of light on a mandarin's desk and Ming-style scholar's cap chair. The unframed painting of Adam and Eve is seventeenth-century Peruvian.

when expanded to three levels with many rooms, still lacked a sense of space. And it was finished! If I were to sell Round House, I could build afresh.

Returning home, I found a note from the architect Ed Barnes apologizing for his late return of a monograph on Ise, the seventh-century Shinto shrine in Japan. I became newly aware of the subtle perfection of Ise's majestic proportions, with massive roofs above buildings raised on stilts. At my new house project, LongHouse, raising the principal floor would offer views over the flat terrain. The tranquillity derived from Ise's wooden buildings would also express the same serenity and long vista as my Japanese loft in Greenwich Village.

Where on the LongHouse acres should I build? The logical place seemed to be an island in the center of the clearings, a still-impenetrable jungle of broken trees and monster vines. By the time my friend Peter Olsen joined me for a late summer holiday, this was sufficiently cleared to set up tall stepladders for a view from the second-floor level. We next built outlines in bamboo of the thirty-five-foot-high gables to envision how the house would look from the land. Just south of the main gable, a lotus pond was staked out to conform to the crossing of the two hemlock hedges. Earth from the pond excavation would be sufficient to build a huge, ten-foot-high berm parallel to the house to provide a garden area at the level of its principal rooms. The balance of the excavated earth completed a twelve-hundred-foot-long berm parallel to Hands Creek Road.

Another advantage of this house site was its location a thousand feet from the road. Again as protection, I approached the farmer, my neighbor, to buy the remainder of his woodland, now five times the price but a fair deal and on good terms. The long driveways were staked out and surfaced, the site leveled, and the pond dug out for a bentonite liner. When this was finally covered with many truckloads of sand, there was the celebration of slowly filling it from several garden hoses.

Originally my idea was to timber the house with logs and to use as consulting architect a Japanese teahouse builder named Jokan, who had apprenticed rebuilding the Ise Shrine. Charles Forberg would collaborate on mechanical matters, codes, and contracts. Jokan worked with us for a time but continued to need an interpreter. When he asked for four Japanese roofers to come for a whole year, Charles and I decided to go forward without him. This became our thirtieth collaboration in which I sketched a floor plan, he provided structure, and together we developed materials and finishes. When Charles suggested that

The large, skylighted living room has space for several seating groups as well as the display of a variety of decorative arts.

Even larger than the main living room, the summer living room below it has three walls open to the garden, providing a cool space out of both sun and rain. Wicker lounge furniture permits seating for fifty. With stacking chairs, two hundred guests can sit for a concert. Basket chairs in the foreground are by Nana Ditzel for Larsen Furniture.

we utilize masonry piers to support the giant roof trusses and stuccoed curtain walls, I responded with the notion of a slatelike roof, made by Monier of Gunite cement.

My original thought was to tile the ground-level floor and use old patinated teak floorboards from Thailand for the main level. When we realized they would not weather well on the veranda and in the plant-filled conservatory, we chose to tile all but the minor wing. To satisfy my desire to employ the full-length vista so successful at the New York loft, Charles proposed a breezeway bridging the long main wing and the minor wing, which is set at right angles to the main wing but twenty-four feet away. This gable would pierce through the minor wing to form the north-court portico. Similarly, Charles carried the conservatory transept through the main wing to form the open, thirty-foot-high stair hall facing west. My thought had been to continue the stair to the basement level and have a large dumbwaiter between floors. Friends suggested that even if we were not putting in an elevator, we should leave a place for it. We found that with a small, three-level Elevette we could eliminate the lower stair and dumbwaiter and arrive at the same cost.

My timely visit to a new carpet-design studio in Switzerland, built in the A-frame attic of a large old house, gave me the idea that LongHouse would have the potential for another level. With a sixty-five-foot skylight running down the peak of the main wing, there was opportunity for splendid light in a library and large home office under the eaves. Above my long dressing room, a glass-walled writing studio was also feasible.

Frank Lloyd Wright said that the client states what he wants, but the architect provides what is needed. In this case, the architect found a code to limit my quest for mezzanine space and cut off the home-office floor well short of the eaves on either side to provide reflected light into the kitchen and dining room below. He also devised a masterful scheme for wrapping a suspended steel staircase around the open elevator shaft. Working at a butcher-block kitchen counter while I was pondering which hardwood to use for the stair treads and rails, I decided that this same hard maple would provide the lightest color. Ordering the treads precut and finished from the factory proved to be a great saving, cutting down on job time as well.

When the mute swans, Cob and Pen, swam in Peter's Pond, no lilies or lotus were spared from their foraging, nor ladies safe from their advances. Now, with the swans gone, we enjoy glorious blossoms but no water ballet.

Opposite: A view over a partners' desk in the home office and past the small library reveals the vista through a succession of rectangular trusses, which support the weight of the massive roof.

Raised beds of heathers and heaths provide year-round color at the near side of the enclosed lap pool. Beyond it, a white pine allée leads to Claus Bury's homage to the Brooklyn Bridge, which is almost like an eighteenth-century folly at the end of the vista.

Bury's work is composed of cypress pyramids supporting a Cor-Ten steel beam. When dancers from Jennifer Muller/The Works Company performed on the sculpture, their movements intensified the static/dynamic characteristics of the piece.

Savings of both time and money were necessary. Long-House had been planned when our company yielded handsome bonuses and dividends, but when it was built, I had neither. When Round House finally sold, it was for half the expected price. Except for the generosity of Anita Corey, Peter Olsen and I would have been homeless on weekends! Forberg's fast-track plan to design as we built produced good results but was not fast. Four years of planning and construction brought improvements but doubled the target cost.

Spending weekends so close to the work in progress was exciting but frustrating. My father, the contractor, used to tell his impatient clients, "When the roof is on and the windows in we will be one-quarter completed and have spent one-fourth of the money!" True! Suzanne Slesin's headline when the *New York Times* published LongHouse would be "The House That Jack Built, and Built, and Built." I maintained a degree of patience by developing the gardens. This went slowly at first because Round House also had to be maintained. When that sold, we (and the gardener) could gleefully concentrate full-time on the new projects.

Central to the Red Garden, this study in heightened perspective employs parallel rows of cedar posts painted the red of torii gates at Shinto shrines. These diminish in size and height to make Toshiko Takaezu's stoneware pot appear farther away than it actually is. In May, azaleas in various reds reinforce purple plums and red barberries to create a resounding clash of fiery hues.

Dale Chihuly's Crystal Gardens, which premiered at LongHouse in 1996, was the artist's first environmental work created for the landscape. Primarily blown in Nuutajärvi, Finland, during the summer of 1995, groups of large asymmetrical glass forms were installed in the gardens, in the pond, and as chandeliers suspended from oak trees. This was just prior to Chihuly's famous installation of giant chandeliers along the canals of Venice. Here his fluted forms emerge from the ground like the fronds of a giant fern, rising to catch the sunlight.

The first project was planting the large berm by the house. The southwest slope had been spread with topsoil to receive a dozen ground-hugging plantings in large drifts, including four cultivars of spreading juniper. The south side was studded with beach plums; the north and east slopes were covered with sand for dune grass, except for a broad band of santolina, lavender, and other drought-tolerant perennials near the steps. The flattened berm was paved with crushed brownstone and a heavy table installed, and this place overlooking the pond, the house site, and the developing terrain became fine for lunch breaks.

When the mason asked for five thousand dollars to haul away fill from digging the basement, more berms on the site of the original meadow seemed a reasonable course. As I was now seldom at the beach, we could create sand dunes here. It took but a short time to form, contour, and cover them with tons of sand. Then the planting began. Silvery santolina and gray cypresses were added to dusty miller, fine-stemmed grasses, and *Rosa rugosa.* Packed-down gravel paths led through these dunes to the steps up the house berm, to the motor court, and out to the lawns. In only a few weeks we were well started on a major, one-acre garden feature.

The other projects took more time and money, except for the rocks. In Holland, as the tale goes, St. Nikolas leaves rocks or coal to bad boys at Christmas. For years I was given boulders from the sandpits of a friend who owned the bulldozer! In summertime at LongHouse today, these hundred or more no-maintenance anchors are not very visible. But in the planning phases, half-buried boulders (so rare on Long Island) were significant landmarks. Between these outposts we laid out the trees, shrubs, and border material that would define the garden.

The cryptomeria allée along the entrance drive also went in easily. Although these forty ten-foot-high trees arrived half-baked on a hot May day, they responded so well to a watering emitter on each tree as to grow quickly, even in their first year – so quickly that in their third year I decided to move every second tree to the north boundary. These twenty-foot trees responded to the tree spade without a whimper. Both groups now reach skyward, becoming each year more noble.

The next great allée came about incongruously, when the lap pool, so carefully envisioned to run the length of the summer living room, seemed as though it would be too shaded and cold. Instead we moved it to be on axis with the west gable and the raised heather garden. Needing enclosure, we ran wire fencing within a privet hedge for the two long walls, with double-hinged

Between the rose garden and the soft fruit-and-vegetable cage, Augustus Saint-Gaudens's golden Diana shoots straight down a long hemlock hedge. From August onward she is framed by peegee hydrangeas; earlier in the summer she is partially clothed in tall white roses.

cedar gates across the narrow ends of the pool. Between these walls a long bluestone terrace is enlivened by a perennial border reflecting in the fifty-foot length of the black pool.

When the German sculptor Claus Bury came from Frankfurt, we decided to rebuild his *Homage to the Brooklyn Bridge* at the far end of this axis, almost to the property boundary. We screened it with drifts of leafy bamboo except along the sixty-foot side facing the house. As the wide, two-hundred-foot-long grass walk to the site called for sheltering borders, I selected Eastern white pine as an evergreen foil for some maturing beech trees in the area. The result is both a strong cross-axis to the length of the house and an architectonic reference to it.

On this western side of the house, the old lawn was graded to create a level croquet court north of the lap pool and a square lawn south of it. Both are bounded by the hemlock hedge on one long side and informal island beds of conifers on the other. At the first "Trees as Art" auction I found a giant weeping blue Atlas cedar trained to spread horizontally on a single limb about ten feet above the ground. With this tree placed across the north end of the croquet lawn, the effect became a gray-green Niagara. The bluish color, so often reading as outlandish, is ameliorated by a trio of standard blue Atlas cedars towering above the nearby hedge and a wall of blue spruce and silvery autumn olives behind it. The highly satisfying result is a level, lush green panorama on the western side of the house to contrast with the dry, sandy berms on the east.

The breezeway overlooks the sunken rose garden, which blends a wide range of perennials, flowering bulbs, and ground covers with clematis and climbing roses. Winter interest is augmented by a birdbath and a thistle-seed feeder attracting such choice small birds as finches and cardinals. The oversize terra-cotta pot is a classic amphora.

The pond has developed slowly. At the near end, four Korean cherry trees reflect in its waters. At the far side, two fine Japanese cherry trees – without the grafted trunk so common in America – are a graceful relief from the staccato verticals of pondside iris and tall grasses. The hardest day of my life was probably the one spent lifting heavy lotus and lily plants out of the ponds at Round House for planting in the shallows in the new gardens next door. Alas, the young swans thought we were feeding them. Within days the blossoms and leaves disappeared; in a week there was no trace of stems. The lotus pond became a swan pond!

From the second-floor veranda, with the advantage of some elevation, it seems as if half of the LongHouse grounds can be surveyed (above). The view across the pond and first lawn takes in the pink garden, with its repeating verticals of white birch trunks. Beyond it stands a collection of maple trees chosen for their magnificent fall color. In this photograph Grace Knowlton's copper forms create a frieze at pondside. The trees above them are Korean flowering cherries. The view toward the house (opposite) shows Knowlton's masonry forms in the foreground.

Among the successes in creating winter interest on the grounds of LongHouse is the "waterfall" of cascading branches of the weeping blue Atlas cedar. Toshiko Takaezu's tall black stoneware form also serves as a focus of the hornbeam allée.

In addition there were the mallard and Muscovy ducks attracted by daily handouts of swan food. If the swans had continued to perform their water ballet all this would have been acceptable. They did not! At the time when their young wings had been clipped, what nick in those webbed black feet would have curtailed movement across the lawns? As it was, they became increasingly aggressive in chasing after people, with every intention to bite. They attacked the tractor mower with special vigor; watching the driver charging swans with a broom may have been the comic joust of all time! Another gardener went to the clinic with a swan-mangled thumb. I supported the swans' territorial rights until the end of the third summer. Three pretty, downy cygnets with pale lavender plumage hatched that year to happily swim in single file behind Mother. Then, one dark night a fox ate the baby swans, pillaged the Muscovy nest, and carried off Mother duck. That was it! When I found out that the remaining swans, like other bullies, were cowardly when actually confronted, they were carted off to a distant lake.

The building exterior sufficiently complete, we began to concentrate on the areas contingent to it. Like Ise Shrine, the house was to sit on a rectangular pad of coarse gravel. This would separate it somewhat from the plantings and serve as a catch basin for rain from the steep, gutterless roof. Under the gravel, from the two-hundred-foot tiled walk west of the house

Wisteria vines were trained up steel cables strung well in front of a windowless two-story stucco wall. Especially in winter, they cast dramatic shadows.

Although LongHouse now boasts fifty cultivars of bamboo – including several less than knee high – this golden yellow groove bamboo from Korea is most common and totally evergreen. Their invasive runners are easily moved to areas where tall screening is desirable. Note the ground covers (here Rochester ivy and Virginia creeper) that form an understory below most plantings.

As seen from the dune garden, the entrance gate is both the ceremonial passage into a private world and – especially for the LongHouse Foundation – a means of controlling traffic.

to the berm on the east, heavy vinyl sheeting carried the runoff to French drains leading into the pond. Between the walk and the hedge I laid out four rectangles of sunken gardens to be surfaced with the same stucco as the house. A white garden the length of the plaza in front of the pond has proved to be a great success, because no voles have entered to eat the white tulips and Casablanca lilies flourishing there.

As the various heathers and heaths have year-round color, we planted them in a raised rectangle consistent with the west gable, where they are visible from three levels of the house. Connie Cross of Environmentals, who selected them, asked that we plant them in two feet of sharp sand, preferably grit, and never fertilize or water them. Having previously pampered heathers as they slowly declined, I was delighted to see Connie's formula working. The same harsh conditions are employed in a smaller rectangle within the heather beds. Below grade, a thyme lawn of six prostrate species planted in sand between mossy rocks also prospers.

In contrast, the sunken rose garden opposite the breezeway is fed and watered frequently, producing fresh color from the first snowdrops until the last rose blossoms at Christmas. The northernmost of the rectangles is a soft fruit-and-vegetable cage sunk thirty inches below grade and screened five feet above. The black mesh covering keeps birds and squirrels out of the raspberries and protects the lettuce and herbs in the center bed from rabbits.

The fifty-foot-long summer living room at ground level has proved to be a breezy oasis in hot weather. The sun is glorious on the tiled plaza between the house and pond, with wafts of perfume from gardens on either side. A fine view of the pond is interrupted only by the profile of a granite fountain, square in plan like the lily pool below it. Hand-hewn by a family friend when I was only eight years old, it appears to have been designed for this space. Bathing birds believe its large, shallow basin was carved for them, and the water trickling into the pool fills the air with gentle music. Towering above the fountain are two masonry piers matching those of the house and supporting the two halves of a broken pediment. Architect Forberg, who conceived this heroic device to relate pond edge to house site, named it the South Gate.

The other gate is the main entrance, set within a hundred-foot stucco wall parallel to the house and separating the outside world from the privacy within. Just south of the gate and its sheltering gable is the Gate House, partially supported by the long wall. Within the gate, the austerity of rolling sand dunes provides another separation between the lush woodland outside and the masonry of the massive house beyond.

Strike the great bronze bell to announce your arrival! Ascend the broad steps of the berm before the house to enter a sheltered world of terraces and water gardens. Move across the wisteria-draped moon bridge into the conservatory, a plant-filled transition between the interior and the gardens around it. Welcome!

Our most admired garden feature is this allée of stately *Cryptomeria japonica* from the roadside berm to the gatehouse turnaround. Other than wanting some additional water in droughts, it is totally maintenance-free – a quality all too rare in this or any other garden.

I am just as curious as those who ask me why I am so drawn to amassing objects

of many kinds. *Obsession* is probably as descriptive as *possession*; anything worth

having is worth having in extreme. At the point of acquisition lurks the feeling of

gaining approval because of ownership of the object, as the Southern mountain girl

sang, "If I had a ribbon bow, my love would think me fair." ■ I also recall my

response to the natural self-possession of certain African-American soloists in the

Alvin Ailey dance troupe, wearing only pants, but so self-assured they were totally

in control of the space they moved in. It seemed that if I had what they so naturally

possessed, I would have everything and would want nothing more. Without such a

sense of completion, extraordinary or unnecessary objects seem to fill a void.

Both the similarities and distinguishing features of these spouted pots become more apparent through juxtaposition. Note the various solutions to spouts, handles, and lids. Although we most associate these shapes with tea, in earlier times they more frequently held wine or oil.

Probably it all started with parents more comfortable asking friends to "come to

Two vignettes from the 10th Street loft show how well these lighted glass shelves, with fabric-wrapped boards behind them, display a variety of objects. The "black-and-white department" (above) uses this color limit to relate pieces in all media. Primarily East Asian ceramics are grouped on the shelves on the opposite page. The most valuable piece, the fourteenth-century Thai lusterware plate (center), was bought for a song on a Philippine island, where they had no idea of its origin or value.

Jack's garden, or Jack's menagerie" than "come see Jack." Certainly my formative mind would have thought that way – not in the showing-off phase, but, while collecting, some vague anticipation of approval. Although I delighted in receiving gifts, letters, and valentines, the pieces themselves had less fascination than bees captured in my bare hands, tadpoles and frogs, seedling trees, shells, and snake skins. Relating to others through shyly sharing such collections was a pleasure, but it was the act of acquisition that proved to be irresistible.

Stamp collecting, of course, was different, as it involved research into the countries that the stamps came from and a lively competition with my friend Malcolm Peterson, whose collection always exceeded mine in certain directions, but not all. Marguerite Murphy would send me first issues and always exotic, beautiful stamps that would be any collector's pride. I preferred the large, inexpensive assortments of European stamps that had to be sorted by country, with duplicates for trade, then put into the books in an orderly fashion. Who were all those crowned heads from faraway places: handsome King Carol of Romania; the deposed Hapsburgs; Emperor Franz Josef, who magically evolved from a young boy to a corpulent old man?

Later on, collecting phonograph records was just as mind-expanding. After I had all the popular swing platters, I moved toward operettas, tone poems, and program music. Here were haunting lyrics and melodies, pounding through my head until I could hear them again and learn their rhythms. A cousin arrived with a great hoard of Edison cylinders, including all the great old operatic arias. That this strange device made sound at all was something of a miracle. By a stroke of great fortune, I inherited a hundredweight of early twelve-inch records, each a quarter inch in thickness, heavy and fragile, but with the glorious sound of Scotti's and Caruso's early-twentieth-century classics. In time, I tired of the most accessible music to enjoy more Baroque music, especially Bach, and Gregorian chants.

While working for a Dutch florist at fifteen, I was urged on by his enthusiasm for the best of music. Although Saturday afternoons were always our busiest time, there was to be no talking while Texaco's "Opera on the Air" played in the back rooms of the shop. As we wound stems and trimmed arrangements in silence, he led us on with a pantomime of scorn for notes missed and enthusiasm for favorite passages. Soon I had recordings of a number of the operas and chances to attend the San Marco Opera matinees in Seattle. In 1944 the most exciting part was watching the lineup of Italian workers with all of their two-dollars-a-week pay, buying balcony seats on Saturdays. Their good-natured enthusiasm, as they sang roles from Verdi or Puccini, expanded my awareness of a romantic Old World.

Near the end of undergraduate studies, when I had given up worldliness for an inner life with more meaning, I achieved some sense of sharing and immediacy. Stripping the decks of adolescent follies and passions, what was more meaningful than possession? About the time I had given away everything but the clothes I was wearing, I took a spring semester screenprinting course with Ruth Pennington. As the season brightened, she would come back from country weekends freshly tanned and in wonderfully becoming new summer dresses. For fabric-design students to see this effect of color and pattern simply cut and becomingly fitted seemed a gift to us — not vanity, but sharing. In thinking about this, it seemed clothes and possessions that had an art quality were beyond vanity.

I was also inspired by three other great teachers at the university. The first was Hope Foote, our great professor for interior architecture and the only one who successfully imbued taste. At a time when we longed to be part of the design revolution and to paint with bold strokes, as we defied the past to strike out in new (or seemingly new) directions, she was a stickler for the detail of honed refinement. "What do you mean the chair is red? Which of a thousand reds?" I learned from being in her apartment and sharing her collections of furnishings and objets d'art, textiles, and designed objects, many of them brought back from China and Japan. Many were aids to entertaining, such as presentation dishes that made even simple foods appear grand. She encouraged our enthusiasm, saying that even if we found one beautiful object each year, far beyond the ordinary and with durable association, we would soon have some lovely things to live with. I knew this to be true, but felt an acquisition once a month, or once a week, would go faster. And so, I collected.

On Saturday mornings I would make a tour of the downtown thrift shops at St. Vincent de Paul, the Salvation Army, and a wonderful shop in Japantown to seek out Indian baskets, which at that time regularly came on the market from turn-of-the-century attics. Not the largest or the best ones, but fine, small examples from the Aleutian Islands, Oregon, and British Columbia. Usually these were twined of spruce or cedar root and imbricated with lustrous strands dyed with berry juices. I learned something about their technique and the people who

In addition to every window at LongHouse having a particular view, interior walls are compositions. Here in the living room, Kozimon's drawing of the Siena Cathedral hangs above a classic Chinese temple table, a multi-layered basket by Dorothy Gill Barnes, a shaman's box from Mindanao, and footed bowls from East Africa.

Opposite: A setting for an autumn buffet: the cloth is a West African tie-dye, the baskets are from the Philippines, the lacquer serving bowls are Japanese. The two footed bowls by Gerry Eskin are among dozens I have gathered because they add glamour to even the simplest foods. The old bottles holding grasses cost next to nothing.

made them. It was a wonderful small collection. Benefiting from my familiarity, I closely examined the great examples at the ethnographic museum.

Our design instructor, Mary Bassetti, who had worked with Marcel Breuer, Walter Gropius, and Frank Lloyd Wright, knew something of the modern world beyond the Northwest. Her house was full of treasures reflecting that world. There were such utilitarian pieces as Prestini's turned wood bowls, modern stemware, the best of the new stainless flatware, porcelain and stoneware plates, fine lamps, and some chairs by famous architects. When I asked Mary how they afforded all this, she explained simply that she did not have the sterling silver, Baccarat stemware, fine china, and chests of linen damask that young women were expected to slavishly protect. She had collected what was meaningful to her and her simpler, more individual lifestyle.

Margaret Hosmer was an extraordinary woman who had left Tidewater Virginia for the Broadway stage. After marrying a handsome Bostonian, she helped found the Institute of Contemporary Art in Boston. When her husband was called out to work on the atomic-energy plant in eastern Washington, Mrs. Hosmer began teaching lifestyle courses at the university. She opened up the eyes of a generation of coeds to the life beyond the conventional norm. With great drama and enthusiasm she communicated passion for the special, but also the commonsensical. After showing a stunned audience her slides of all the great design of our time, and aspects of the past relating to it wonderfully well, she would end by saying, "But of course, if acquiring these objects would mean not being able to afford great music in the house, or putting the baby off a year, then that would be folly."

As her own office happened to be next to the weave studio where I spent so much of my time, I could hear her booming voice counseling students. First she would explain how the hope-chest accoutrements could be traded off to acquire modern dinner services. A few months later, the same girl would be asking Mrs. Hosmer how to be rid of the "square" man that she no longer cared to spend her life with.

From these living examples, I concluded that for most of us collecting would be a manner of focusing on the special and unique, often subsidized by exclusion of normal necessities. Art that was useful, even on occasion, was particularly valued. And giving up some lunches and movies to acquire an object seemed

Ethnographic baskets from dozens of cultures are hung on a twelve-foot-high cedar wall to create a lively low-key relief. Such an assemblage is within the limits of every purse.

to enhance its worth. Then, as now, the characteristic common to my acquisitions was not luxury, nor even quality in a usual sense, but their existing outside the conventions I knew. Whether Edwardian or primitive, Oriental or ultramodern, my acquisitions seemed to reinforce my own personal identity. Never allowed to brag or dominate, but not having learned the charm of humility, in collecting I found a quiet means of sharing enthusiasms.

I also learned from my friend and classmate, interior designer Ted Herried, when he bought two hundred acres of coastline on Lopez Island. After the land investment he could afford only his priorities, not necessities. The cabin he built there was accessible only by a long trail barely passable by car, and had neither electricity nor plumbing. A gas tank fed the refrigerator, stove, and heater for collected rainwater. Gaslights were as romantic as the privy, which was open to the sky and surrounded by small pines except for a view out to sea. There was art appropriate for such a retreat, books, and music. The change from city conveniences became a plus, raising the question, "What are necessities?"

These thoughts were with me as I set up housekeeping in New York. Shopping in New England antique stores provided salad bowls, cutting boards, coffee pots, and all such things. My many trips abroad and my friendship with craftmakers completed an extensive battery of props for serving food and beverages. Some were art, some old or new craft; some were only serviceable. But almost none of them were ever high style or pretentious, which ensured their working together so well.

I never intended to collect fabrics. Through my Peruvian friend, Chan Khan, I acquired some Pre-Columbian pots and fabrics that have been like old friends ever since. Others came my way as gifts or on travels. When Win Anderson and I discovered the richness of pattern-resist fabrics being produced in Nigeria, there seemed no choice but to buy examples of each. My visits to Morocco, Peru, Guatemala, and Mexico were even more productive, but nothing compared to the Indian and Afghan tours. Soon we had a special room for the "treasures," a means of sensibly storing them.

When I was only twenty I met Virginia Harvey of Seattle, a weaver, scholar, and conservator who later worked at the Seattle Art Museum and the University of Washington. There she developed the Harvey System for textile conservation, in which work is not to be pawed through in tissue-lined drawers, as it had been up until her time. Instead, research is done through files or master books containing photographs and full descriptions of each piece. The pieces themselves are rolled over a tube between layers of acid-free tissue, sealed to keep out dust and moisture, and tied with cotton tape, leaving a two-to-three-inch window to reveal the color and nature of the fabric. This is one way to be certain that a given piece is exactly the one that must be opened or loaned without opening the package. These fabrics are then suspended on rods through the tubes in an area of even temperature and humidity.

This system not only protects fabrics, but also reduces staff time considerably, as scholars are free to use the files unassisted. With collection data moving to computer monitors and the capability of enlarging photo images and showing comparative ones, plus cross-referencing, enormous strides have been made. As retrieval of textile collections becomes consistent internationally we have, in one lifetime, witnessed a major revolution. I was both surprised and delighted to find the Harvey System in use in European museums, including the Kremlin.

In my research for my book *The Dyer's Art* and the accompanying exhibition, I became increasingly troubled with museums numbering holdings by date of acquisition. While we could access all library material in the same way, museum holdings were obscured behind dissimilar clouds. By the time Betty Freudenheim researched my *Interlacing* book and exhibit, we were sufficiently concerned as to propose a simple, logical classification system that created hierarchies for all types of fabrics. As a case study, we recataloged the twenty-five hundred textiles in my collection at the design studio; the result was a revelation. Suddenly cards with photographs of batiks from every culture were contiguous, so their differences and similarities could be studied. Or, by collating provenance keys at the end of each catalog number, all Japanese examples were identified. With some determination to solve the problem on an international level, my LongHouse Foundation is at work proposing such a decorative-arts classification, using its relatively small, extremely diverse collections as a case study.

Returning from an extensive world trip about the time *The Dyer's Art* was published, I took solace in knowing I would not need to acquire more resist fabrics. Nine major dealers were waiting for me in New York because publication had only

A Dick Wickman table top makes a fine landing strip for a diverse collection of teapots, mostly from East Asia. The black one in the foreground by American designer Peter Saenger accommodatingly warms four cups.

The view from the LongHouse veranda across the plaza, with the south gate pillars and lily pool, toward Peter's Pond. The bamboo sculpture is by Roy Staab, the granite fountain by Ed Anderson. I brought back from India the large Ming Dynasty pots at bottom left.

revealed my susceptibility. As I no longer needed quantity, I only bought the best, the rare, or to fill in gaps. At the same time I was building collections of contemporary crafts, notably small porcelains and basketry. I understood, for the first time, the meaning of being a collector. For me, at least, it meant raising or borrowing acquisition funds, then storing what I had so recently purchased. It seemed as if spending money on hand to fill available walls or shelves was only decorating. As I learned to deacquisition pieces of considerable value, those large or fragile, or near duplicates, I realized that continued ownership was no more essential than forever listening to the same music or poetry. When my Bernard Leach pots seemed too formal, they made suitable wedding gifts.

I learned that the connoisseurship involved in collecting is also a responsibility. Collectors are temporary guardians. As collections usually do not pass down within a family, they either come back on the market or are given to museums and learning institutions through charitable gifts and bequests. A responsibility of a collector is the choice of a final destination for the collected material. Some museums are collecting fiber responsibly, with conservators and support staff, but others are lax in this area. I try to give where the material will augment rather than duplicate collections, and where it will be cataloged and exhibited or published.

The serious connoisseur upgrades collections and is intent on acquiring the best examples, even the rarest ones, in a given category. This should be especially true of contemporary material. Making good choices requires knowledge gained by studying correlative material, catalogs, and monographs.

When collections leave our hands, will they be better or worse because of our stewardship? Fiber of all sorts, including works on paper, is particularly vulnerable, as is its color. Sunlight is especially destructive, but so is light of all kinds. So are soil, pollution, contact with most paper – and people. Above all, we might learn from the notorious Collier Brothers, who never threw anything away and died trapped by stacks of periodicals, that not discarding is not the same as collecting.

A guest at my recent seventieth-birthday party wrote, "Love your home and gardens. I can see that you have spent a lifetime collecting art, craft, and friends." Yes, I have collected friends, perhaps more selectively than any of the objects, chosen for their interests and their willingness to put up with my foibles. Having friends in one hundred cities around the world is my greatest wealth. Each year I lose some, but not really. Like the high points in the books I have read and the performing arts I've experienced, they are always with me.

Purchased from Dale Chihuly's Crystal Gardens exhibit at LongHouse, this *Niijima Float* is remarkable for its marbled surface, including light-reflective gold dust. With an earlier, almost black companion, it stays in the dune garden winter and summer, when we enjoy the counterpoint of lyme grass the same color. As collectors run out of room indoors, art for the garden becomes increasingly desirable.

CHAPTER 6

Mentors

AILEEN OSBORN WEBB

Aileen Osborn, Mrs. Vanderbilt Webb, was a strong, handsome, kindly woman of a certain mind-set. I first met her in 1951 and came to know her in a close, working friendship lasting until her death. The last time I saw her was over tea at her penthouse. When I said I would visit again, she demurred, "Don't be sure: all my affairs are in order; my brothers and I are so decrepit we will all go soon – foom, foom, foom!" And she did, her enormous energy spent. She had never quite recovered from a broken hip nor from the powerlessness of an expended fortune. Only in the very last years had she not been able, by force or resource, to will her visions into being.

I remember her otherwise in some proud moments when she accepted blithely our tributes to her contributions, and when she made her threat/promise to spend weeks at Haystack Mountain School's old site at Liberty, Maine. Our director, nervous about the extended visit of so imposing a matron, asked me to vacate my room next to the downstairs bath at the faculty house. I was to move to the other downstairs bedroom and go

Laying the cornerstone for the Museum of Contemporary Crafts (later American Craft Museum) in 1955, board members of the American Craft Council surround our founder and chairman, Mrs. Vanderbilt Webb. Left to right: architect David Campbell, Walker Weed, Mark Ellingson, Kenneth Chorley, Aileen Webb, William Barrett, myself (with new mustache in an attempt, at twenty-seven, to appear older), Richard Petterson, potter Antonio Prieto, professor Arthur Pulos.

upstairs to shower. He also built a temporary wall that would screen her room and private bath. On the first Sunday night, when we gathered around the fire to discuss events of passage and qualms of start-up, the young Colombian graphics instructor who – because of Mrs. Webb's visit – had been moved up to the third-floor attic complained of mice keeping him awake. Aileen immediately and determinedly offered to switch places; she slept so soundly that mice would not disturb her! Only with considerable difficulty did I dissuade her. Already in her late sixties, this outdoorsy woman proved a good sport; when one of our Thursday cookouts was abysmally fogged in by a cold, dark wetness, she organized the men for a lively game of inner-city stickball.

I learned from her the value of persistent determination and an adult level of drive quite different from my boyish one. One fine fall day her country neighbor, Russel Wright, and I were to join her for a twelve-mile trek from her house to Russel's. As there was no path, the tortuous route atop the foothills would take us there. At one point she said, "You boys rest here; I will run the dogs!" Russel, considerably her junior, and I (still in my twenties) happily accepted a breather while Aileen and the dogs leaped from crag to crag.

Even in the formative mid-century decades Mrs. Vanderbilt Webb was not the mother of the American craft movement, at least in the sense of giving birth to it. Somehow this dynamic and pervasive uprising would have happened without her or the institutions she founded. But without her energy, craft would certainly have evolved differently, more slowly, and would probably have been more closely tied to grassroots regional traditions still predominant in the 1940s. Nevertheless, she most certainly mothered the evolving growth of interest in craftsmanship, first in the craftmakers themselves, then, slowly, in collectors, and finally by broad marketing, ranging from street fairs and craft shops to the major art galleries across the country.

It could be argued that Aileen Webb was in the right place at the right time, but in what ways right? New York, in the postwar years, seemed halfway between America and Europe, as if Manhattan were the island of Bermuda. In many ways, it was an unlikely place for the founding of the American Craftsman Council (now the American Craft Council) and the American Craft Museum. Except for the designers and artisans in the fashion industry, there has been little craft focus in the city itself,

whereas there have always been craftsmen, collectors, shops, and galleries in other areas and, importantly, major colleges with influential teachers in other regions. However, New York is important as America's marketing hub and publishing headquarters.

Aileen was a magnificent autocrat, tireless, determined, humane, ecumenical, and fun-loving. She embraced all of craft worldwide. The library/boardroom at the first Craft Museum boasted a stained-glass wall with the motto "Trust Those Who Work With Their Hands." She had this trust, more than most. In this room we often sat through luncheon board meetings. Aileen ate quickly, then picked up her small gavel to win the approval of her well-hewn agenda. Neither old-family appointees such as Dewitt Peterkin and Kenneth Chorley nor the otherwise vocal designers Dorothy Draper, Dorothy Liebes, Edward Wormley, and I opposed her. Why should we? The Council expressed her vision and her wealth.

Most of us had sat at the meeting in which Ely Jacques Kahn, architect of record for the Seagram Building, came in late and all smiles. When his client had decided there would be no bank or store on the street levels of Mies van der Rohe's tower for Seagram's, he had proposed the Craft Museum. This space (which became the Four Seasons Restaurant) would have high ceilings, great lighting, superb detailing, and its own entrance. Mrs. Webb's response, "We will not be in that whiskey building," closed the discussion. I don't know why. Even brief meetings at the museum started with a poured glass of sherry; there was no opening without a whiskey bar. Perhaps Mrs. Webb knew that Seagram's largesse would come with a board voice stronger than ours.

Only twice did we oppose her. When the America House lease ran out in the old CBS Building, I suggested we abandon this subsidized craft shop in favor of broader craft marketing. The America House loss of money was substantial, and relations with craftsmen were strained by the inherent conflict between goals of helping craftmakers needing to sell and presenting only the finest work. Mrs. Webb persisted, buying the brownstone at 40 West 53rd Street, rebuilding it handsomely, and installing *Craft Horizons* magazine (now *American Craft*) on the upper floors and a new America House below. However, this brought the same result: when attempts at wholesaling and commissions proved even more costly than retail, she began to complain about the competitive offerings of American craft at Bonnier's and Georg Jensen, support which the Council should have celebrated. As the last gasp and with a typical Webb blooper, Aileen protested that the closing "would kill the goose that lays the egg." But when the vote was tallied in favor of closure, she offered this improved real estate to the Council for one dollar. It was with this building, in a hold-out position against CBS expansion, that we obtained the present condominium space for the American Craft Museum.

In the same boardroom Mrs. Webb laid the groundwork for the American Craft Council's sponsorship of a new effort, the World Craft Council. The board responded, "When we have yet so much to do at home, how can we even consider taking on the world?" Unabashed and with the same patience, she engaged Margaret Patch to start up the WCC with the ACC serving only as the American entity, not the umbrella sponsor. As long as Aileen was alive, the WCC had considerable success in bringing out better understanding of craft leaders in the developed and developing world, in fostering national craft organizations, and in hosting magnificent meetings in New York, Lima, Kyoto, Dublin, Toronto, and Istanbul.

"Where can we go?" she asked me in the later years. "I want one more adventure before I die." When I suggested taking a jeep across the Sudan from Dakar to Lake Chad in central Africa, she was enthusiastic. Only her breaking a hip prevented it. Pity! She would have been a great traveling companion.

EDGAR KAUFMANN, JR.

When I first met Edgar Kaufmann, son of the Pittsburgh merchant and philanthropist, he was director of the Good Design shows at the Museum of Modern Art, which was almost single-handedly carrying the banner of modernism across America. After a successful program of opening eyes, minds, and doors through many exhibits and small books, with titles such as *What Is Modern Art?*, *What Is Modern Architecture?*, and *What Is Modern Design?*, Edgar launched a five-year program of exhibitions. The influence of these Good Design shows reached beyond the museum to the Merchandise Mart in Chicago and department stores such as Bloomingdale's and Carson Pirie Scott. The net cast was broad, including mass-production pieces readily available, the main line of modern furnishings, and a few handcrafted prototypes, including mine.

Of all the people who helped along the way, Edgar Kaufmann, Jr., has had the most enduring influence. His writings as design chief at the Museum of Modern Art instructed me while still in school. Although we remained good friends for forty years, he was still an enigma, with more comprehension of "how things are" than I will ever acquire. We also shared a protective shyness, even with each other. Although this chasm was more often bridged in later years – like a shaft of bright light deep in a cave – I was always concerned for his sensitivity.

From our first meeting I found Kaufmann intensely personal, informal and democratic, upbeat and inclusive. He was also shyly sensitive, brilliant, thoughtful, generous, very rich, and well educated. His being overawed by a powerful father and namesake, while being less than robust in physique and not handsome, must have been a handful. For years we were shy and, perhaps, overly considerate of each other. In 1957 when I was vice president of the Architectural League and hosting a dinner with Philip Johnson as speaker, I invited Edgar as my personal guest. My thinking was that with their shared time at MoMA, they would be old friends. Edgar's response was, "Don't you think the last day of March, save one, could be better occupied?" It turned out these contemporaries with much in common were lifelong adversaries: it was because of Philip that Edgar quit the museum. I became even more cautious with Edgar.

My "walking on eggs" attitude changed through a curious sequence. One morning the phone rang early. It was Alexander Lowen, the founder of bioenergetics therapy and my therapist. He canceled my morning appointment but asked if I could come around 6:30. I said that would be fine, as I had a dinner party nearby at 8:00. With Dr. Lowen I went through exercises to invite vulnerability and experience breathing deeply as a way to tolerate momentary discomfort. On arrival at Edward Benesch's penthouse, I found my mentors there, including Edward Wormley, Mrs. Vanderbilt Webb, and Edgar. For the first time I felt comfortable greeting them as an adult and equal. The social pain (if any) would be only momentary. After dinner Edgar (who would usually leave as early as I did) and I fell into such a deep conversation that our hosts went to bed. We left with the staff after 1:00 A.M. The next day, when I had a call from Edgar apologizing for keeping me so late, I explained to him how my new openness came about.

After the next dinner at my apartment, I must have been nodding over coffee, for he wrote, "You sleep so hospitably." When I remarked on this, he said, "Jack, you must do as Mother did at Fallingwater. She would call out to my father, 'Edgar, we must go to bed now so these nice people can go home.'"

Because I was usually at Haystack Mountain School in the late summers, I had not visited Frank Lloyd Wright's masterpiece when Edgar went there every August. With my Japanese friend Hideho Tanaka, I spent Christmas week with Edgar on the isle of Hydra, one and a half hours offshore from Athens. I had wondered why he would travel so far from Park Avenue to a treeless city lot in Greece. Although the port is densely built and arid, in fifteen minutes we could walk out of it to open land bursting with cyclamen and lilies. One entered Edward's walled forecourt to find that the rock had been replaced with deep, clear water for swimming, and the plant-filled verandas on the upper floors had a fine view of the harbor and its historical buildings. Because pirates based in this port had defeated the Turkish fleet in the war for independence, the Hydra residents paid no land tax. We had a fine time.

EDWARD WORMLEY

I met the famous designer Edward Wormley during my first autumn in New York. He had sent an assistant up to my studio asking if I would weave a special drapery for a model room. Woven in a melange of golden yarns, it was called Cornsilk. Later he used my fabrics from Thaibok on the furniture he designed for Dunbar. In 1954, when we started printing cloths, he was our first and best client. He liked the modern, allover quality of the patterns and the solidity of our color. All through the next decades he remained our top client and favorite sounding board as we listened to his avuncular advice. The admonitions became all the more valuable because he could support them with orders.

Several times each year Win and I visited him in the spacious living room next to his office. We laid out samples and strike-offs over the chairs and sofas to visualize designs out of the studio, and in use. Almost all our screenprints were introduced at Dunbar, as well as a number of wovens and handwoven blinds. When Edward took exception to a new pattern with exotic birds, I asked why. "Because birds bring babies and our clients don't want babies." When I reminded him that birds had been popular on fabric since the Renaissance, he responded, "They were for dukes wanting successors and farmers needing help. They *wanted* babies." On another occasion he warned, "Don't use bedroom colors at your living-room prices!"

I thought that Edward had designed an ideal lifestyle for himself, one I would try to emulate. Beyond the entrance to River House, the luxurious apartment building at the end of East 52nd Street, one entered a small door to a minuscule lobby, then descended two floors in a private elevator to a garden-level lobby. One bell there was for Edgar Kaufmann's rectangular block with glass walls facing a garden. Another was for the

Wormley apartment, and a third for Edward's compact offices. Dominating the first office was Helen, a six-foot-tall former Ziegfeld Follies dancer who was now a benign monarch we could all depend upon. In the days before faxes, one would phone Helen to ask, "Would Mr. Wormley like to . . ." Or, she would call saying, "Mr. Wormley would like . . ." Within earshot Edward could see Helen's desk through an open door to the studio, where he worked from a tall drawing board overlooking the garden. Behind him, assistants and draftsmen were out of his sight but within earshot. Meetings were conducted in the apartment, which was located through a long art gallery and included a huge space with glass walls on two sides and such large trees that it seemed a garden room. If interrupted by a phone call, Edward could disappear into his telephone room. Upstairs were expansive private quarters, including his aged mother's apartment overlooking the garden.

One day Edward called to say he was having a large gathering and, as some of his staff were ill, he asked if I could loan him my housekeeper, Ida. I acceded gladly, thinking that when Ida saw how much space Edward had, she would feel more sanguine about doing work for me. Ida came in the next morning complaining that Mr. Wormley had four in-house help, and all I had was her!

Edward and I sat together on the American Craft Council board and attended the same openings and parties, including his. For the black-tie award evenings Win and I were soon double-dating with Edward and his guest, ducking out a little early for cabaret at the Blue Angel or another popular spot. When we left them there at 1:00, I wondered if I would ever be old enough to party into the wee small hours.

I spent the fifties wondering whether I could be saintly, like Haystack's director, Fran Merritt, or at once worldly and earthy, like Mr. Wormley. Edward was sixty-two when Dunbar was suddenly sold and he took too-early retirement in Connecticut. When I asked him if he would design furniture for our company, he said, "Jack, if I wanted to design for anyone, it would be for you. Fortunately, I can afford not to." Years later, when I asked for the third time, he accepted, saying, "My lawyer says I should be paid up front; I'm too old for future royalties." We agreed, and although his hand-colored renderings were handsome, our sales staff felt they were too much like the era just past. Our Wormley Collection never went into production.

Small in stature, mischievous, both earthy and worldly, the late Edward Wormley was one of my mentors and a great early influence. Others would lead by example, open my eyes, and open doors. With his flourishing interiors practice and as a designer for Dunbar Furniture, Edward could back his preferences with orders – instructional indeed!

BERTHA SCHAEFER

Although I have never thought of Bertha Schaefer as a mentor, I was certainly her protégé, her "discovery." By the time she first visited my New York studio, I knew her interior-design style from a tour with Hope Foote of a fine house Bertha had done in Seattle. She asked if I would design some things for her next exhibit. Would I create an upholstery for her new sofa design? And dense window blinds for a lobby with an abysmal outlook? She was also the courageous art dealer for a number of fine painters and artist-craftsmen such as Wharton Esherick. When I first encountered the Bertha Schaefer Gallery, it reflected her broad interest in combining walls for painting with Gothic tables and special appointments. On occasion she would introduce artists who worked in craft media, such as the embroiderer Mariska Karasz and the weaver Trude Guermonprez. The gallery decor changed after the painters insisted on a neutral white space, and when Bertha branched out to introduce Esteban Vicente and the first postwar Spanish painters, then British sculptor Kenneth Armitage and his circle.

Soon I was her occasional escort and sole guest at her rented beach house in the Hamptons, where we were participants in the active art scene on the Artists' Beach and at the constant parties. Bothered by the mating dances of dealers, collectors, and Abstract Expressionists, I was consoled by Saul Steinberg, "Jack, this is nothing new; it was the same in Paris when Cubism was young."

All the while I marveled at Schaefer's unique work method. Well aware that most interior-design clients enjoy being deeply involved with their projects for as long as possible, Bertha would simply invite them to her office to audit the proceedings. For whole afternoons they watched and listened as Bertha dealt with gallery artists, editors, museum curators, the people on her staff, and designers for this and other projects, including myself. All this provided a unique education that resulted in most of her clients becoming rather knowledgeable collectors. Several years after we had worked together with the owner of a large house, I asked her about the client. Bertha told me that our client had continued to collect and was now herself painting, a little disappointed that she had not been invited to show at the gallery.

I assumed my adoption was temporary, and that soon Bertha would have a new protégé. This was not so. Instead, we were friends for the rest of her life. The last time I visited her at the hospital before she died, she asked that since she had never built any of the houses planned for her East Hampton property, could she remain at Round House? I agreed. She left others the land, her savings, and the collections. I inherited Bertha's ashes.

STANLEY MARCUS

Of the men I have known well over considerable time, few have impressed me as much as Stanley Marcus, long ago adopted as the big brother I missed in childhood. His achievements as the legendary merchant who transformed luxury stores, his direct involvement with the majority of today's sales catalogs, and his hand in civilizing the cow towns of Texas: these are well documented, especially in his own books. I have known other successful men, some of considerable virtue and amazing minds, but with Stanley I continue to be amazed at his wise understanding of people, his forgiveness of human foibles, his caring and compassion. Polite and punctual, he seems to stumble less on minor setbacks than the rest of us do, as if stalled traffic only gives him pause for reflection, or a puppy slow to learn exercises an opportunity to learn patience.

I remember so well our first real visit, in the 1950s at the downtown Neiman Marcus store. On his invitation I stopped off in Dallas on the way home from Los Angeles. At dawn the night plane put down at Love Field in almost one hundred degrees of breathless humidity. About ten that morning there was a frosty blizzard. Mr. Stanley explained that Dallas, neither contained by hills or forests nor blessed with a great lake or river, was wide open to storms sweeping down from the plains. Furthermore, his city was not enriched by cattle like neighboring Fort Worth or oil like Houston. He long ago realized that if anything would "make" Dallas, it would be its development as a trading center.

After we shared enthusiasms for mutual friends in far-off places, he invited me to see some of his "discoveries" in the store. At his brisk pace I traipsed after him, noting how he could greet staff as we passed by, pick up litter, and straighten gloves on the counter without breaking step or losing the thread of what he was explaining. His staff salutations were personal, like, "How's that baby?" Without waiting for an answer, he smiled, waved, and was on to our next destination. His respectful regard for a new stock clerk reminded me of a child's story about the young George Washington: when asked why he bothered with such amiable civility to his grooms, George explained that civility was the price of his privilege to have grooms. Although no patsy and intolerant of anything unfair, Mr. Stanley is a kind man. Those he meets are innocent until proven otherwise.

We would visit a showcase for which he had considerable enthusiasm. This could be his introduction of fine jewelry or Bohemian crystal, "truly of a collector's quality but, because of current exchange, a superb value." His belief is that if innovations are properly presented and explained by knowledgeable sales staff, the man in the street will consider their purchase. This reaching beyond expectations was gamesmanship, in which he often won. So did his customers and staff. It all reminds me of the Broadway lyric popular at the time, "See the pretty apple on top of the tree. Up, up on your toes!" Stretching to the top of our abilities was all he asked of us – and of himself. Part of his stretch (and mine) is keeping on top of diverse projects and correspondence with not just friends in four corners of the globe, but all those others who write in with requests and inquiries. Mr. Stanley arrives at early breakfast each morning having dictated responses to these letters so his decks are cleared for dealing with the day ahead. His punctuality often permits the briefest of replies, often spontaneous and from the gut, making his task that much easier.

The mature Stanley I now know is sufficiently well rounded and forward thinking to not lose equanimity under pressure. He welcomes risk as long as there is a fall-back position. At board meetings I have observed his thoughtful silence while others play out their opinions. When Stanley finally speaks, we all prick up our ears to better understand his sagacious suggestions. Like a great general, his advice is typically, "It's true, we are surrounded, but it seems our best chance is to feint with our left flank, then break through with our right." I have seen similar responses in dogs on a tether. Young hunting dogs strain so much at the end of the leash that they can't spring forward if they need to. Older and wiser dogs drowse near the stake, knowing that they have the full length of their lead available, and all their endurance.

My adopted big brother for four decades, Stanley Marcus continues to inspire with curiosity and energy that keep him young and with an easy-going consideration for everyone he meets.

I have still not learned to emulate Stanley's ability to luxuriously, languorously revel in the present after catching up with required tasks. At his home in Santa Fe he will say, "What do we most want to do today?" What freedom! It reminds me of the summer vacations from school, when I could still ask that question. Now my options seem limited to doing either the most urgent or important things first. With sadness I have learned that the first options done may be the only ones completed.

My own practice of these priorities leads me to stress the importance of vocation to young people. Now you have the energy for fun after a full day of work, but before long, you won't. Then it will be even more important that your work is your pleasure, and if it is, you will excel in it, providing satisfaction. Perhaps you will achieve a level of fulfillment that creates magic, and because there is so little magic in this humdrum world, others will be drawn to it, hoping some will spill over on them. Take risks!

This memoir began when Abrams publisher Paul Gottlieb visited LongHouse to announce, "I want you to write about design and craft, collecting, houses – all those areas that interest you most, including gardens. And yes! Explain how you go about planning a garden."

Of course, this is *not* all. Sadly omitted are my many friends, the staff members I have worked with all my life, and the special family this only child has adopted over the years. Many of these are working relationships toward some end. If I once envied painters their being able to work in solitude while

Afterword:

And That's Not All

I was dependent on many, I learned before long that the studio and the larger Larsen organization were unknowingly created as an extended family, in which I would be both looked after and listened to. I thought then of the company as a child we must all tend and nourish. We did, but that child was me. That these relationships are personal and need not be shared here makes them no less important. What I have achieved was never accomplished alone.

So there is little mention of the five sisters who have been important to me, or the two big brothers, and spare mothers, or the other special people with whom I have shared life. Missing, too, are the causes I've supported and, in some cases, instigated. Haystack Mountain School is only briefly mentioned; the American Craft Council hardly at all. I joined that stellar board in 1955 as the towheaded kid. Later I was president and historian, then moved over to the much expanded American Craft Museum. There are still many board and committee memberships, and causes and concerns for design education, for quality, and for what often seems like the demise of civilization. Discussion of the essays and lectures, the juries and benefits, is not here. Nor did I elaborate on my involvement with LongHouse Foundation, embracing a whole complex of causes.

For many of these organizations I cannot be a key contributor, but rather pass on the fruits of experience and connections to those with similar missions. Sometimes I feel like the central operator of an old-fashioned telephone system: most of all I enjoy making connections! The most telling example of this was with my friend Dale Chihuly. I first met him in Seattle when our mutual professor Hope Foote admonished, "You must help this guy; no one has worked so hard since you were in school." Dale had also majored in interior architecture and then changed to weaving. When we met, he was heating strips of glass sufficiently to bend them over and under to form an interlaced plane. I suggested he learn glassblowing with Harvey Littleton, the father of modern glass, who had been a prolific potter when I was at Cranbrook.

Dale did go to Madison to work with Harvey, becoming his star student, then demonstrating the skills and vision to develop styles quite his own. When he won a $2,000 prize, he came to me about starting a glass school in the Northwest – in tents. I told him to join up with Anne and John Hauberg of the Weyerhauser family, who wanted to build an art center on their tree farm north of Seattle.

This project became Pilchuck, the great international glass school, which John Hauberg, Dale, and I paced off at the tree farm in the drizzle of a November day. My contribution was the experience in building the Haystack Mountain School as an organization, then as a campus. Dale's was an expansive vision. From the start, faculty and students would come from overseas, with budgets far more generous than other summer art schools. Because John Hauberg's conviction and generosity matched this vision, Pilchuck was built with bold strokes that have paid off handsomely. As I told Dale when he, John, and I met in my New York apartment, you must match John's gifts with excellence in all aspects. And he did. The Seattle of my youth was a lumber capital with the Boeing plant. Today it is also the city of software, coffee, and art glass.

Still later I was able to instigate Dale's exhibit at the Musée des Arts Décoratifs in the Palais du Louvre. My friend Mark Tobey had been the first American given a solo exhibition there; I was the second. That the third might also come from Seattle was irresistible.

For sport, Dad fished and hunted successfully. Most of his photographs are with enormous salmon, or dozens of game birds, or a recumbent moose. To me, matchmaking is much more fun. Of course, the best matches are inevitable. Most of them would happen without my intervention. Dale, for instance, is so charismatic he would have succeeded without my small boost. So, perhaps, would have all those others. Still, planting ideas and suggesting connections make for the best form of gardening I know. It's as exhilarating as matching fabric structure to materials to pattern, but on a larger scale – and a very human one.

On the eve of Dale Chihuly's colossal Crystal Gardens exhibit at LongHouse, he was photographed with Peter Olsen (right) and myself. The large, shadowy form in the background is the chandelier Dale made for the three-story stairwell.

Chronology

1951
Arrived in New York City with M.F.A. from Cranbrook Academy of Art. First commissions to weave lobby draperies for Lever House and to design American Random Collection for Thaibok, Ltd.

1952 and 1953
Established Jack Lenor Larsen, incorporated. Designed first powerwoven fabrics and imported first handspun, handwoven fabrics from Haiti, soon followed by others from Morocco, Colombia (Doria), and Mexico. Win Anderson and Bob Carr join firm.

1954
Handprints of Spice Garden Collection offered in first Larsen showroom at Park Avenue and 58th Street. Manning Field and Jo Hertz join firm.

1951–55
Exhibited in "Good Design" exhibitions at the Museum of Modern Art, New York.

1957, 1960, 1964
Reported the Triennale di Milano as guest editor for *Interiors* magazine.

1959–60
Visited Taiwan and South Vietnam as consultant to U.S. State Department to help set up local craft operations; also made first visits to Japan and Southeast Asia. Worked with Edward Larrabee Barnes on fabrics for Pan American Airlines 737 fleet; the new campus for Haystack Mountain School of Crafts, Deer Isle, Maine; and the Larsen showroom on Fifth Avenue.

1959
Designed first stretch upholstery fabrics and first printed velvets.

1959–62
Served as co-director of fabric design at Philadelphia College of Art, Pennsylvania.

1960–62
Designer and director of traveling exhibition, "Fabrics International." Visited West Africa and the Transvaal.

1963
First visit to Morocco. Opened JLL International in Zurich.

1964
Received Gold Medal as design director and U.S. Commissioner, XIII Triennale di Milano.

1965
Created first designer towel collection for J. P. Stevens.

1966
Completed Round House in East Hampton, New York. Wove wall panels for First Unitarian Church of Rochester, New York, commissioned by Louis Kahn.

1967
Retrospective at the Stedelijk Museum, Amsterdam. Visited Poland for the Museum of Modern Art, New York.

1968
Co-curator of "Wall Hangings" exhibition at the Museum of Modern Art, New York.

1969
Designed first fabrics in 747 jets for Pan American and Braniff Airlines.

1968–72
Retrospective exhibitions at the Museum Bellerive, Zurich; the Museum of Fine Arts, Boston; and the Renwick Gallery, National Museum of American Art, Washington, D.C.

1972
Acquired Thaibok Fabrics, Ltd.

1973–76
Five visits to China. Established Larsen Carpet and Larsen Leather.

1974
Designed "Visiona IV" exhibition in Frankfurt for Bayer AG. Silk hangings for Sears Bank & Trust, Chicago, commissioned by Bruce Graham of Skidmore, Owings & Merrill.

1975
Artist-in-Residence, Royal College of Art, London. Toured New Zealand and Indonesia.

1976
Established Larsen Furniture division.

1977
Curator of "Wall Hangings: The New Classicism" exhibition at the Museum of Modern Art, New York.

1978
Retrospective exhibition, "Larsen Influence: The First 25 Years," at the Fashion Institute of Technology, New York.

1980
Designed porcelain tableware for Dansk International. Co-director of "The Art Fabric: Mainstream," traveling exhibition opening at the San Francisco Museum of Modern Art.

1981
Retrospective exhibition, "Jack Lenor Larsen: 30 Years of Creative Textiles," at the Musée des Arts Décoratifs, Palais du Louvre, Paris.

1981–89
President, American Craft Council.

1983–84
Editor, "Design Since 1945," Philadelphia Museum of Art.

1985
Terra Nova Collection designed to support the Museum of the American Indian (for Mikasa, Martex, et al.).

1986–89
Curator of "Interlacing: The Elemental Fabric," exhibition opening at The Textile Museum, Washington, D.C.

1990
President Emeritus, American Craft Council.

1992
Established LongHouse Foundation in East Hampton, New York. Designed carpet, wall and window fabrics, and leather upholstery for Trustees' Dining Room, Metropolitan Museum of Art.

1996
Awarded Gold Medal by American Craft Council. Lifetime Achievement Award, Surface Design.

1997
Merger of Larsen company with Colefax & Fowler Group.

Publications

Elements of Weaving. With Azalea Thorpe. New York: Doubleday & Co., 1967.

The Dyer's Art: Ikat, Batik, Plangi. With Dr. Alfred Buhler and Garrett Solyom. New York: Van Nostrand Reinhold, 1971.

Beyond Craft: The Art of Fabric. With Mildred Constantine. New York: Van Nostrand Reinhold, 1972.

Fabric for Interiors. With Jeanne Weeks. New York: Van Nostrand Reinhold, 1975.

The Art of Fabric: Mainstream. With Mildred Constantine. New York: Van Nostrand Reinhold, 1981.

Interlacing: The Elemental Fabric. With Betty Freudenheim. New York: Kodansha International, 1986.

The Tactile Vessel/New Basket Forms. Erie Art Museum catalogue, 1989.

Material Wealth: Living with Luxurious Fabrics. New York: Abbeville, 1989.

Index

Numbers in *italics* refer to captions.

Photograph Credits

Unless otherwise noted, the photographs are courtesy of Jack Lenor Larsen, incorporated.

Courtesy American Craft Council: 143
Courtesy Win Anderson: 52
Courtesy Baker Furniture: 45, 59
Dorothy Levitt Beskind: 16 top, 23
Gilles de Chabaneix/Maison Française: 99 bottom, 139
Amos Chan: 47
Harvey Croze/Cranbrook Academy of Art: 18
© Todd Eberle: 115, 118 bottom, 132
Plans by Charles Forberg/Courtesy Jack Lenor Larsen: 113
David Frazier: 134, 135
Claire Garoutte: 51
Oberto Gili/Architektur & Wohnen Jahreszeiten Verlag: 121, 136
Robert Grant: 100, 101, 104 bottom right, 105 top right, 105 center
Olga Gueft: 6
Kari Haavisto. Reprinted by permission from House Beautiful, Copyright © November 1985, The Hearst Corporation. All rights reserved: 44
Bill Helms: 30, 39
Lizzie Himmel. Reprinted by permission from House Beautiful, Copyright © June 1997, The Hearst Corporation. All rights reserved: 137
© Elliott Kaufman: 114, 116–17, 120

Jack Lenor Larsen: 74, 75 top, 88, 89
Courtesy LongHouse Foundation (map drawn by Perry Guillot): 112
Sam Maloof: 80
Cutty McGill/1988 U.S. Local Screening for the International Textile Design Contest, Fashion Foundation, Japan: 21
© Herbert Migdoll: 40, 41, 71 bottom, 90, 94, 122 bottom, 124, 126, 126–27, 128, 129 top, 141
© Joseph W. Molitor/Haystack Mountain School of Crafts: 19
Hélène Pancoast: 103, 129 bottom
© Mary Randlett: 16 bottom
Susan Wood Richardson: 28, 104 top left, 107, 108
Karola Ritter: 5, 131, 118 top, 125 left, 131
Courtesy Toby E. Rodes: 33
Paul Ryan/Juliana Balint: 104 top right, 138
Geri Scalone: 68, 69, 70
Keith Scott-Morton/Copyright © British House & Garden/Condé Nast Publications Ltd.: 119, 140
Courtesy Southern Illinois University: 13
Roy F. Staab: 111
© Curtice Taylor: 110, 122 top, 123, 125 right, 130
Roland Terry, F.A.I.A.: 36
Courtesy Thai Silk Company: 66
Horst Thanhäuser: 105 top left, 105 bottom left, 105 bottom right
Courtesy Western Pennsylvania Conservancy: 38, (Kenneth Love) 145

Acknowledgments

To complete a book spanning so long a time frame I am indebted to many, including photographers, editors, and publishers. Friends including Mildred Constantine and Peter Olsen have been helpful, but my constant support team has been Judith Hancock Sandoval, the most pleasant nag I have ever known, who helped me greatly with early drafts and picture selection, and my assistant, Crystal Cooper, who patiently persisted in preparing draft after draft. I appreciated, too, the gentle professional guidance of editor Elisa Urbanelli, and the direct, buoyant art direction of Ellen Nygaard Ford, both of Abrams.